'S No Geese Like Snow Geese...

*Chasing the Wild One and Other Misadventures
in a Lifetime of Wildfowling Fun*

By Jack Hirt

P.O. Box 115, Amherst Junction, WI 54407
www.ihuntbooks.com

0-9721321-7-1

8 24274 22995 6

**This book
is dedicated to
my father, Ken,
who took the time
to get me out there.
And to my wife, Mary,
who understands
I continue to
need to be.**

TABLE OF CONTENTS

Dedication..3

Acknowledgments..6

Introduction...7

CHAPTER ONE:
The Basement Hallway Closet.................................8

CHAPTER TWO:
The Marsh...10

CHAPTER THREE:
Huntin' The Horicon...19

PART TWO:
Expanding Our Horizon..31

CHAPTER FOUR:
Collins Remembers...32

CHAPTER FIVE:
The Lure of the Big Lake...35

CHAPTER SIX:
Canada Calling...40

CHAPTER SEVEN:
First Snows...45

PART THREE:
The Shape of Things to Come..............................50

CHAPTER EIGHT:
The Honeymoon...51

PART FOUR:
The NoDak Years..57

CHAPTER NINE:
Let's Go Joe...58

CHAPTER TEN:
New Blood...63

CHAPTER ELEVEN:
The Pass...67

CHAPTER TWELVE:
Starting Over... Again...69

CHAPTER THIRTEEN:
RVing For Snows...75

CHAPTER FOURTEEN:
Gunning A River of Geese.......................................83

CHAPTER FIFTEEN:
Bread and Butter Wildfowling............................88

CHAPTER SIXTEEN:
Intro to Layout Shooting.......................................90

CHAPTER SEVENTEEN:
Canada's on the Rise **92**

PART FIVE:
Reaching Out **99**

CHAPTER EIGHTEEN:
A Party in Patagonia **100**

CHAPTER NINETEEN:
Hudson Bay ... When Less is More **109**

CHAPTER TWENTY:
North to Alaska ... A Wet and Wild Fowling Adventure **117**

CHAPTER TWENTY-ONE:
A Rice Field Reunion **124**

CHAPTER TWENTY-TWO:
Timber Time **130**

CHAPTER TWENTY-THREE:
Spring Snows ... The Mud, The Blood, and the Gear **136**

CHAPTER TWENTY-FOUR:
Potholin' ... Again **144**

CHAPTER TWENTY-FIVE:
Oh Canada **147**

CHAPTER TWENTY-SIX:
Seaduckin' **151**

CHAPTER TWENTY-SEVEN:
Down Mexico Way **154**

CHAPTER TWENTY-EIGHT:
Alberta Calling **158**

CHAPTER TWENTY-NINE:
Truckin' with the T-man **167**

CHAPTER THIRTY:
Huntin' for the Cameras **173**

CHAPTER THIRTY-ONE:
Gone to the Dogs **178**

CHAPTER THIRTY-TWO:
Ducks for Bucks ... The Dollars and Sense of Waterfowling's Future ..**190**

CHAPTER THIRTY-THREE:
The Guides **195**

CHAPTER THIRTY-FOUR:
On Snow Geese **203**

CHAPTER THIRTY-FIVE:
Looking Ahead **205**

This book would be of no substance
had it not been for those
I've been lucky enough to
share life's time with in
the marsh and field, most notably:
Grandpa Gordon, Uncle Bill,
Warren M., Joe L., Dave K.,
Steve H. and his crew, Hummer,
Brian F., Dave W., Pat P.,
Gus and his boys,
The Schepp family, Steve L.,
Rev. Jim, my sons Bill and Jack,
John D., Randy L., Kevin M.,
Mike L., Jay S.,
and the dogs that have owned me:
Shamus, Sadie, Tanner and Maggie.

Waterfowling, Wildfowling ... call it what you will ... is about everything but killing. Still, the cycle of the hunt is not complete without the taking. That of the harvestable excess.

While shooting birds is a key factor ... and one for which I'll make no excuses ... this book is really about everything else in the world of waterfowl. And in that sense it seems ... though unintentionally ... our place in it.

Volumes have been written by "experts" about what it takes to kill fowl. How to set a decoy rig. How to hide. How to call. Basically, how to fool 'em. The info so proffered can be useful.

But, c'mon!

Here we are, arguably the most advanced, most intellectually evolved critters on the face of this planet, armed with the ultimate in technology. Shouldn't we be able to take these pea-brained birds at will? Especially since it really takes little more than simply putting ourselves where the birds most want to be.

Well, of course we should.

The undeniable fact that we sometimes ... oftentimes ... can't, is wonderful beyond description, beyond explanation.

So, if you want to learn about what it takes ... technically ... to kill birds, this work is not for you.

But it is, I'd hope, for those Everymen who go out there just to be there; and who sometimes wonder, but don't really care why.

I wish I could put into words everything that is so unique, so mystical, so truly special about the pursuit of wildfowl in the marsh and field. But what's truly beautiful is that those words maybe ... heck, likely ... just weren't meant to be.

Each of us, diehard 'fowlers, every one, knows deep down inside that our passion is just that. Something that helps fulfill our souls. Something we just can't live well without.

Aside from my father, my mother, my grandfather, my uncle, my wife, my boys, my grandchildren, and my special friends ... two and four legged alike ... this book is for YOU, my fellow enthusiasts.

Live well. Get out there. Shoot straight. Enjoy. And pass it on.

CHAPTER ONE

The Basement Hallway Closet

My introduction to everything that is so special about wildfowling began, oddly enough, with a closet. Built beyond a youth's reach over the basement stairs, a visit to this sacred vault, I'd learned, was a prerequisite to each of my father's duck hunts.

Come October, I'd watch him each Friday night while he'd raid the closet to ready its treasures for the next day's hunt. Just opening its squeaky door created a sensory overload, as the rich and pungent odor of gun oil and Hoppe's #9 spilled into the hallway.

Once open he'd always reach first for that green canvas, leather-trimmed gun sleeve encasing his trusty old Remington Model 11 Sportsman. As a matter of habit he'd slip the gun from the case and double check that it was unloaded. Then, sometimes, he'd even let me hold the heavy piece as he touched it up with a drop of oil here and there.

Next would come the heavy, military style ammo box. After a quick inventory of its contents, Dad might find the need to tap the closet's stock for a red and green box of Remingtion Kleanbore paper shells, the type he still used on dry weather days, or maybe even one of those prized boxes of the neat new Peters blue plastic 5s, if wet weather was a possibility.

The Hodgman hippers, having been hung by their heels, were then grabbed and turned down in fireman fashion, so they'd be ready to be stepped into, before being set alongside the gun and ammo.

Lastly, he'd reach for his coat of choice. In the early season it would be the standard-for-the-time, lightweight but sun-bleached and blood-splotched khaki-colored, multi-purpose field jacket. But in the late season, with the onset of potentially ice-breaking weather, it would be "The Parka"

he'd reach for.

The parka was a heavy, sheepskin and wool-lined, full-length, army green affair that, Dad explained, he'd been issued 12 or 14 years earlier during his WWII tour of duty on Kiska in the Aleutian Islands. Purposefully avoiding the specifics, Dad made it clear that this coat was special for far more than the mere comfort it provided. It was something I still sensed years later as I made good use of the venerable garment.

As a youngster in the '50s I longed for the day I could reach that closet. Finally, come one memorable day in 1961, I did. Barely able, while stretching out and up on tiptoes, and under Dad's watchful eye, I managed to pop the latch. As the door swung open, much to my amazement, there stood a second gun case leaning up against Dad's. With my jaw no doubt hanging wide open, I was too hopeful to even ask. But when I turned to see the smile on his face, I knew. That cheap, shiny vinyl case could have been Corinthian leather for all I cared. And the low budget 20 gauge Mossberg bolt action it held was, to this day, the most beautiful gun I've ever laid eyes on. Far more than a mere gun, it proved the key, opening the door to a lifetime of wildfowling adventure.

CHAPTER TWO

The Marsh

Every lifelong waterfowler has his roots sunk deeply into that one special locale on, or in which he was first introduced to our special sport. Mine are forever stuck in the boot-sucking muck of eastern Wisconsin's Sheboygan County Marsh.

In the beginning "The Marsh" was my whole world of waterfowling, just as it had been for my father Ken, and my Uncle Bill Gordon. A full half hour drive through the country from our north 12th street home in Sheboygan, just motoring west to the Marsh with the duck green aluminum 14 footer in tow ... the all around craft of choice for area sportsmen at the time ... was a major journey. One, when made at 4:30 a.m. in the toasty comfort of the backseat of the family sedan, that indelibly burned the era's rock and roll tunes, invariably blaring on the car's a.m. radio, deep into my groggy, semi-conscious mind. (Roy Orbison "grrrowling" Pretty Woman comes prominently to mind)

But those early adventures made a lot more meaningful impressions as well. The optimistically spirited hustle and bustle at the boat ramp as hunters jockeyed their rigs for position. The cold, dark boat rides that seemed to last a half-hour, but in reality were 10 minutes at most. The teamwork involved in fishing those crummy, old, often broken-beaked paper mache decoys out of tattered, half frozen burlap bags; then carefully placing them in a classic fishhook pattern. And waiting those last five agonizing minutes until legal shooting time, while the best flights of the day strafed the rig. These things and everything else that is wonderfully unique to our sport were instantly and deeply ingrained, setting the hook on what remains a burning passion.

Those first couple duck seasons with Dad and Uncle Bill thor-

oughly dominated my sporting year at the time. Whether playing ball, fishing, or while at school, (certainly while in school), there wasn't a day in my life, (not unlike now), that I didn't think about ducks or duck season. Yet in reality, since my dad and uncle had to split time on that third seat in the boat with my cousin Billy and I; I probably didn't get to hunt more that 6 or 7 times each of those first few years. Our fathers could hunt only weekends, and then not always both days. Dad and Uncle both did physical labor, and though it was hard for a youngster full of piss and vinegar to fathom, they really needed the occasional day of rest.

In reality, the majority of our Marsh hunts would have to be characterized as slow at best. Though I thought it perfectly natural, even acceptable at the time, the fact is the place got a lot of pressure. The challenge for any Marsh hunter sadly, was to not only deal with the less-than-abundant amount of birds, but also to outfox, outhustle, and sometimes even outrace the competition to the best spots. Any day you got a little shooting, or even better, took home a bird or two, was a good one. Still, though they were far and few between, we experienced some real standout hunts as well.

Opening days ... if you secured your spot a minimum of six hours before the noon start, and were able to successfully guard it ... provided reliable, if not spectacular shooting. The first opener I experienced came during my second season. I drew the lucky straw because Billy, the far better athlete, was playing freshman football that Saturday. Just minutes before the long-awaited opening gun I felt something like a lit match touch the back of my neck. My first kill of the day was the nickel-sized bumblebee I swatted in response. Swelling neck and all, I killed my first duck barely five minutes later. Hopping up on the middle seat to be able to shoot over the tall, waving, still green early season tulies, I took the right-to-left crossing greenwing cleanly. Totally mesmerized by my prize, I couldn't put it down until Dad shouted, "Here's another one!" In a nearly unconscious reaction I jumped up to dump the drake woodie that had used the same deadending flight path as had the teal.

Two shots. Two birds. Man, did I like it! Two-and-a-half boxes of 20 gauge

6s later ... a sobering dose of reality if there ever was one ... I finally finished my four-bird limit with a bluewing, and an ugly black and blue mark stretching from my elbow to my ear. It was a badge of honor I'd proudly wear in the gym class locker room the following week.

Though maybe not the ultimate in quality, the Marsh and the hunting it provided was all we had and all we knew. If for no other reason than we were willing to put in the time and work at it, the Red Gods continued to smile on us from time to time. The Great Redhead Shoot being one of the most memorable of those.

During my entire "career" to that point there had been closed seasons on redheads and canvasbacks. But that year Redheads were fair game. It mattered little to us however, because we'd seen very few while hunting our bread and butter bluebills and ringnecks. And it was that usual brown, black, and white fare that was on our minds as my Dad, occasional hunting partner Warren Mitchell, and I set up a diver spread on the big lake portion of the Marsh that late October Saturday morning. Shooting time came and went, but all remained quiet in our boat as a bright sun burned its way into the cloudless, azure sky. With the bluebird conditions several other groups packed it in early. As they powered across the open water, one of them kicked up a medium-size flock of ducks that had been hidden among a raft of coots. Their wingbeats were those of divers, but it immediately struck us that they appeared bigger than usual. Only when they flashed high overhead, fully lit and in clear focus, could we see they were "Redheads!," as we hissed in unison.

There was no good reason why those birds liked our rig more than the several others on the lake that morning, but they did. After swinging wide on their first pass, they banked hard and confidently, as redheads often will, then bored straight in. I'd graduated to Gramps' old 12 ga. humpback that season, and was happy to have its firepower as the three of us came up gunnin'. Now, I'm sure there were a few hens in the bunch, but apparently none of us had seen 'em. To a man, we'd concentrated on "color." When the smoke cleared we had six stone dead drakes ... our limit ... bobbing among the decoys.

Now, Warren and I weren't even decent shots at that time of our lives; but Dad was exceptional. Though he insisted to the contrary, I'm sure he tripled. Mitch and I, due to some unusual good fortune, had teamed up on the rest. But no matter, we all thoroughly enjoyed our trophy moment. Once in hand we took time to admire our work. Warren remarked, "One or two of these birds would sure look great on the wall." And they no doubt would have, but taxidermy was something that didn't fit into any of our budgets.

By the next year, no doubt due to the combination of evermore-inconsistent gunning, disgustingly heavy hunting pressure on his beloved marsh, and advancing age, Dad started to throttle back. So I found myself spending the majority of my hunting time with like-minded buddies. Warren had gotten his driver's license that year and could occasionally borrow his Dad's '59 Merc wagon. Dad, God bless him, trusted us with his rightfully prized boat.

It was the last day of the season, a bitter cold, subfreezing, early winter Sunday. Dad had sternly warned me the night before, "If it's frozen over, forget it and turn around." As we pulled into the parking lot, only the second rig behind a solo hunter deciding what to do, we found the Marsh was tight with what appeared only a thin layer of skim ice. We hung around, just kicking at the frozen gravel until daylight. But when we first heard, then glanced skyward to see a wedge of divers streaking out over the glass smooth, freshly frozen water, a plan began to form.

"Just back the rig out onto the ice in the landing. We'll see what happens." I suggested to Mitch. Finally accomplishing the feat, something easier said than done with the stone-crushing, power steering-lacking vehicle; our third accomplice Tommy Martin, and I watched as the less-than-one-inch-thick ice first bowed, then fractured under the load. The three of us waded in then, picked the bow up and swung it around, pointing it marshward.

Now, I'm blaming my decision on Dad. It was his fault that he'd told me those glorious tales about times he'd set the boat on plane, effectively putting the entire hull to the task, easily crushing shell ice. Given the power of the new 20 horse Merc Dad had upgraded to that year, I figured we could do it too. So we loaded up. A few tugs on the ripcord and the motor coughed to life. I goosed the throttle and we were off on our noisy way. Man, what a racket, as acres of sheet ice shattered under our high-speed advance.

We wanted to hunt on the west end of the lake but as we approached it, we found the ice considerably thicker. To be sure we didn't wreck any equipment I slowed to an idle, and we used the oars and push poles to first punch out a simple, circular hole for the decoys, then beat and chipped our way the last 20 yards into the rush-lined shore.

It was a full two hours past legal shooting time when we finally reached for our guns, but only seconds late for a small flock of blacks that caught us with our pants down, in Warren's case, quite literally. I was still fumbling numb-fingered with my gun case when I looked up to see the birds first splash into the blocks, then almost instantly explode in a flurry winged departure. We cussed our misfortune as only rednecked teenagers can. Tommy promptly and correctly offered "Aw hell, we'd probably have missed anyway!"

After a short, silent wait a trio of ringnecks gave us a flyby. We emptied out in a three gun salute, but only one hapless bird faltered, finally cart-wheeling a hundred yards off, punching its own hole in the ice on impact. It was a situation that was not atypical given our still lacking level of competence with a scattergun. But it was one that set the stage for the day.

There weren't many birds around, but those that were, were ours. For the first and last time, we had the Marsh to ourselves. As I recall we ended up with 6 or 7 ducks, a mixture of ringnecks, 'bills, and butterballs. But we had plenty of shooting! It was the amount of shooting, not necessarily the number of birds in the bag that more or less defined our success in those early days. Pulling the trigger was godawfully important!

Still, it was a bird we didn't bring to bag that I remember most from that icy hunt. We heard it first, then spotted the drake whistler winging our way on a line that would take him directly overhead. As it did, though it was probably a little high, we opened up. The big, chunky duck never missed a wingbeat, even though its snow-white chest instantly sprouted what would certainly be an eventually fatal, crimson-striping leak. It was a lost bird ... a waste ... but a lesson in the ethics of shooting and hunting that was well-learned.

Shooting finally closed on the day and the season. We'd taken a few birds. And that was great. But more importantly, we'd conquered some hardcore conditions. So we were feeling pretty good about ourselves as we once again broke reformed ice on the run back to the landing. Feeling good that is, until we found Dad parked at the ramp. I waved to acknowledge him. He only nodded straight-faced in return.

I took it as an ominous sign that he chose to stay in the car with Mom while we pulled the boat. As we set about loading gear into the back of the wagon, Dad slowly pulled over to us, cranked down his window, and casually asked, "Have a good day boys?" Warren and Tom were nervously silent as I feebly answered, "Ah ... Yeah ... it was a great one actually." "Well that's good ... darn good. See you back home for supper," he replied with a grin that filled me with relief. And that, thankfully, was the last I heard of it.

The many experiences and misadventures the marsh provided were nothing if not educational. But none were more so than our one and only run-in with "Popple."

Glen Popple was the area game warden at the time. And though I'd never met him, his reputation as a no-nonsense, hard-nosed enforcer of the game laws preceded him. All I knew for sure was that I didn't want to tangle with the guy, and neither did my Dad or Uncle.

It was an early November Saturday morning, one that was shaping up to be another in that season's cursed run of bluebird days. Jetting overhead, their pinions shredding the thick, damp, still air, the birds caught us off guard, streaking in from behind. First bombing for the lake's surface, the knot of 30 or so divers then banked hard, flaring for a little altitude on a comeback turn. It was as pretty an aerial maneuver as a hunter could ever hope to see. Reacting instinctively as the lock-winged flight swung high over the blocks, backlit by the blinding sun just then breaking the plane of the horizon, we cut loose. Only one bird ... an unusually large one ... tumbled. As it did we first sensed we might be in trouble.

"Is that what I think it is?" Uncle Bill asked in a hushed tone.

"I'm not sure," Dad countered, "but it might be a can."

Canvasbacks were closed that season.

Stepping out of the boat my uncle gave us a shove as Dad and I worked the duck-billed push poles. Gliding up to the duck, I swallowed hard. It was a gorgeous bull can. Part way back to our hide Dad chucked the bird to my uncle who, without hesitation, flung it as far as he could back into the cattails. We literally couldn't afford to get caught with that bird.

It had been an honest, but still inexcusable mistake. All was pretty quiet, if fairly tense, in the boat for the next few minutes. I for one, was darn near sick to my stomach. But at least it appeared we were in the clear. Until, that is, a Grumman sport canoe came putt-putting around the corner.

"Oh Jeez," Dad muttered softly. "It's HIM. It's Popple."

Shutting off his outboard, the warden, almost casually, paddled up to our blind, his big, white-chinned black Lab appearing ready to pounce, holding down the bow. With a band of short-cropped, silver hair sprouting below the well-worn, faded khaki duck hat, and a sober, expressionless look on his weathered, leathery face, there was no doubt he meant business.

"Mornin' boys," he began pleasantly enough. Then he introduced himself, as if he'd had to.

"How's the huntin'?"

"Ah ... er ... ah ... well, we've had some shootin' but ... " Dad started, but was interrupted by the warden in a timely, intentional manner, before he could finish. Before he could confess, or tamper with the truth. Before, at any rate, he could put himself in a totally uncompromising, situation.

"Mind if I get a look at your licenses?" came the follow-up question.

After no small amount of fumbling we produced the paperwork, and as he studied it, without looking up, Popple mentioned offhandedly, "You boys should know we've got a bunch of cans on the marsh right now. They came in a coupla' days ago." Then he glanced up and looked ME in the eye, winked, and in a calm, reassuring manner offered, "Keep an eye out for 'em. You don't want to be shootin' any by mistake."

Point made. Point taken. Scared shitless, I only nodded in the affirmative.

Then, with a sly, knowing grin, he simply bid us "Good day!," and slowly motored off.

Sweating bullets by then, we couldn't believe our good fortune. There was no doubt the warden had witnessed the whole scene. And if he'd wanted the evidence with which to pinch us, his Lab could certainly have provided it.

Now, I'm guessing that the good warden, (hardly the bad guy local lore would have us believe), recognized us as the simple, honest sportsmen we were. To say we were impressed with how he handled the situation would be putting it mildly. Ticketing us, even though we clearly had it coming, would still have left a bitter taste in our mouths. One that could have wrongly soured us on the sport. Instead, he took the opportunity to teach us a lesson that's stayed with me the rest of my life. Did he do his job? Oh yeah ... and then some!

The Sheboygan Marsh is still there today. But like so many special places of our youth, it's overused, abused, and not what it used to be. But like a lot of sportsmen of my era, I'll be forever thankful it was there when I needed it most.

CHAPTER THREE

Huntin' the Horicon

*F*or anyone much younger than me it may be hard to believe in these, the good old days of goose hunting. But back in the '50s and '60s in our part of Wisconsin, harvesting a goose ... "A" Canada goose ... was truly something special. Oh there might be a bird or two randomly taken on the Sheboygan Marsh each year. But stories of such feats were usually more rumor than fact. And there were always a few guys fortunate enough to spot and successfully sneak a feeding or resting flock coming off the Lake Michigan migratory corridor. But for eastern Wisconsin's typical stay-at-home duck hunter, a Canada goose was a trophy that, with luck, would come along once in a wildfowler's lifetime ... unless that is ... he got a chance to hunt the Horicon.

Back then, as it still is today, the strictly federally regulated hunt in the Horicon Zone was based on a quota. When "X" number of geese were harvested, whether over the course of several weeks or only a few days, the season was closed. The rich guys, or the lucky guys, depending upon how you looked at it, hunted "the zone" by leasing farmland on the edge of the refuge where they could shoot one bird per day. The average Joe applied through a highly subscribed lottery, for an assigned date in one of the blinds managed by the USFWS that ringed the federal portion of the marsh.

I think I was 12 or 13 years old when early one evening, while still dressed in his house painter's work clothes, I watched Dad's work-weary eyes light up as he tore open the government-brown envelope. "The

Hunt," for my Uncle, Gramps, and Dad, "is on for two weeks from Saturday," he happily announced.

And what a glorious early October day it proved to be! It started out kind of foggy and gray as I pedaled the old Schwinn downtown early that morning for the weekly check-in of my paper route at the offices of the Sheboygan Press. Fat with my $5.50 payday, I made my usual stop at the Kresge store soda fountain to treat myself to a Cherry Coke. Stepping outside after sucking the last drop of juice from the crushed ice; I found a bright sun fast-burning through the remaining haze, lighting up the full-colored maples lining the streets and avenues along the ride home.

All of early autumn's splendor aside, my mind and heart was with my three heroes. Oh, how I wished I was with them! I was anxious too, thinking it would be at least late afternoon before I'd learn how their hunt unfolded.

As I wheeled into our drive I was totally surprised to find Dad's Chevy already parked at the garage. Pulling into the backyard I was greeted with a sight I'll never forget. With Mom's back to me as she squinted through the venerable Brownie's viewfinder, there stood the three proud hunters.

Dad and Uncle Bill, both broad shouldered, meat and potato-bellied six footers, dressed alike in their Jones-style duck caps and gaudy flannel shirts that contrasted mightily with their tattered hunting coats and hippers, were the bookends in the scene. Gramps, skinny, a bit shaky, and definitely showing his age, dressed in buckle galoshes, faded blue work bibs, flannel shirt and trademark turtleneck, and topped off with his always nattily side-cocked Kromer, was the meat in the picture's sandwich. All three had a thick-necked goose grasped firmly in their fist, and were grinnin', it occurred to me, not unlike kids at Christmas, as they posed for the camera. They were obviously enjoying the first-time-ever experience and the special memory they'd made.

Their story still thrills me today.

After a tense pre-dawn drive through a thick ground fog they finally reached the refuge headquarters, and got directions to their assigned blind. Both Dad and Unc kept close tabs on Gramps as they made their

UNC   GRAMPS   DAD

way, still under cover of darkness, through a field of muddy corn stubble. Once situated on the bench of the simple, open-topped box blind; they settled in to await first light and eventual shooting time, still shrouded in a misty blanket of low-hanging fog. Judging by their gabbling, the geese, and plenty of them, weren't more than a half mile away. Excitement built as the guys' gray world brightened and the distant goose music built to a fever pitch, eventually exploding in a deafening roar ... one unlike anything they'd ever heard before ... as the first flights took wing in a thunderous rush. Then they were surrounded by a world of geese, audible, but still unseen. As the birds' powerful wings thrashed and ripped at the heavy air; their resonant calls set the hunters' guts on edge.

There was gunfire in the distance. Then more birds winging overhead, still invisible. The sun finally started to brighten their gray-shrouded world and the cloak of fog started to lift, relaxing its heavy grip on the damp earth. The hunters almost couldn't believe their hard-strained eyes as a trio of honkers simply materialized, quartering toward them well within gun range. It happened so fast there was no time for discussion.

Without a spoken word, the three rose in unison. Their guns sprayed loads of deuces skyward. And all three geese folded, smacking the stubble D.O.A.

It was with true awe that the guys humbly recounted the dreamlike sequence.

I pursued more details about the shooting but couldn't get any. Dad and Uncle Bill did the real damage I suspect. But they never did say. Gramps, quite poor of both eyesight and hearing, was living large that day. Something that was rare for the proud but failing oldtimer. No one was going to chance ruining his time in the sun.

––––––––––––

My first real crack at Horicon came a couple years later. Dad had once again drawn a blind. Only two gunners were allowed, and then with only six shells each. Shooting hours were from 9 a.m. until 2 p.m.

Dad insisted on taking my younger brother, Jerry, along. Since Jerry wouldn't be shooting, Dad, being the silver-tongued devil he thought he was, figured he'd have no trouble talking the feds into making an exception to the two-man rule.

Wrong!

It was touch and go with the guys at the refuge headquarters, and I was nervous. Dad was getting pissed and I didn't want him to blow my opportunity. It was close, but the head-shaking feds finally relented. Little brother could tag along IF we kept him outside of the blind. Dad was still reluctant, but grudgingly agreed. I was selfishly distraught.

From daybreak until 8:30, inspite of Jerry's persistent squirming, wave after endless wave of geese sailed low over our blind. The shooting, had it been allowed, would have been easy, even for me. But come 9 a.m., the bright blue Indian summer sky was completely devoid of geese. We loaded our guns, but with only two shells each, though for apparently no good reason.

It was nice enough sitting around on the calm, unseasonably warm day. The great lunch Mom had packed helped pass the time, as did the impromptu sport of swatting late season mosquitoes. But as far as getting a crack at a goose went ... well ... things looked bleak.

At the start of our last hour a few birds finally started to stir, pretty much just trading back and forth over the waters of the nearby refuge. But then the odd single, pair, or small flock would turn and head out to feed, some passing temptingly close to our hide. Those six shells were burning a hole in my mind's pocket, and I started pestering Dad. "Heck, let's at least give 'em a try!," I moaned.

With but 20 minutes to go he finally relented. I was first to take a whack at 'em. But all I got was quickly rid of five loads. Dad tried some long crossers twice, but disgustedly came up empty, giving me an "I told you so" look each time.

As if in a football game, we were down to two minutes on the clock when magically, a Kamikaze single came winging by low from my side. I fired and whiffed again. For me, it was game over. But Dad instantly followed, rocking the then climbing goose with his first shot, then crunching it solidly with his sixth and last shell, sending it crashing into the tulies 60 yards off. It was a shot of shots.

Jerry was off the ground, trotting after the goose. Though younger, even then he was far faster than me. Yet, I managed to sprint past him, running on adrenaline no doubt, in time to throw a full body tackle on the still heads up goose.

Though not mine, it was definitely "our" prize.

I was at once happy and disappointed. As I went to bed that evening, with the indescribable but wonderful sounds of 100,000 madly honking geese still throbbing in my brain; I remember it occurring to me that the real good news was that I still had my first honker to look forward to. And I was fine with that.

Another two years passed before I got drawn for a tag that would allow me to hunt from a rented blind on private land nearby the refuge. The waiting lines for the best of these blinds were always long on weekends. So, with my parents' permission, my new driver's license in my pocket, and Gramps riding shotgun, I punched school that weekday morning and headed toward Bill Jenkins' farm along highway 49.

We were plenty early that day and had the pick of the litter as far as Mr. Jenkins' blinds were concerned. Having observed it doing plenty of business on a scouting trip the previous weekend, I promptly chose the hilltop blind.

Given the wind that day, I realized too late that it was the wrong choice. The geese ... a lot of geese ... were passing low over the blind down on the flat. The late-arriving hunter who occupied it had his bird in no time.

We continued to stick it out but to no avail. I was getting pretty uptight when the stranger motioned for us to join him. Gramps was always sort of a loner and really not too hot on the idea. But after a little pleading he reluctantly agreed.

The guy was really overly friendly as he slid to one end of the blind to make room. I took the other end with Gramps uncomfortably stuck in the middle. After seeing our "friend's" gun was still locked and loaded I asked him why. "Well, I thought, (hoped was more like it), that you might need some help lad. Be glad to back you up if you'd like," he replied.

Not a man of many words, and not one who could even hear another's real well, the fire still burned in Grandpa, who piped up loudly and clearly in response. "No he doesn't, and he wouldn't like!" Much younger and not expecting such an emphatic response from the oldtimer, the stranger frowned, but wisely kept his mouth shut.

Anyone's first goose is a memory-maker. Mine was a life-changing experience. Angling toward us from the southeast, the loner tried to pass at 35 to 40 yards. I could see its breast muscles flexing as it pumped overhead, then watched as the load of #2s cut a swath of gray feathers just behind the black of the neck. The 9-pounder slapped the frozen earth with a resounding thud, short-hopped, and lay still. By the time I'd tagged the goose Gramps, no doubt as relieved as was proud, he was out of the blind with all of our gear.

Savoring the moment, obviously, had not occurred to him. It was special though, in that it was the last day Grandpa Gordon and I ever spent afield together.

By the late '60s the Canada goose population boom was officially underway. Getting a tag for the Horicon Zone became a matter of simply applying. Something we routinely did. That Horicon outing was always a welcomed addition to our waterfowl season. One often shared with relatives and special friends. And one of those was a special lady named Mary.

We'd just began dating and were having a lot of fun, not the least of which involved her willing introduction to the outdoors. Though never having been exposed to the blood sports, she had enough Tomboy in her to quickly adapt to handling fishing gear. And it didn't take long for her to get up to speed on the skeet field either. Shooting the lightweight 20-gauge auto we'd picked up for her, breaking 18 out of 25 clays on a regular basis qualified her, we felt, for a crack at a goose.

It was a cold, nasty, drizzly, late October Sunday afternoon, as we once again took up our positions in Mr. Jenkins' hilltop blind. If there ever was one thing Mary never was suited for, it's the cold. That being the case, she was layered to the max, topped off with a blue, military-style, hooded parka.

My hunting buddy at the time, and still good friend today, Dave Kovacic, had tagged along with us. Known for his not-always-so-witty one liners, Dave had to remark, "Some camo that is! You tryin' to look like a 'puddle' or what?"

Normally unflappable, I could see the humor was lost on Mary that day. After a slowly soaking hour and a half wait for the evening flight that had yet to materialize, I thought it best to pull the plug. "Maybe we'll try a better day," she suggested gamely.

I cut my college classes the next Friday and Mary took a day off work. That beautiful, warm, and breezy autumn afternoon found us in a remote blind on the east side of the marsh, without any company!

Given the pleasant conditions, we were in no hurry, but a few early birds were on the move. Mary was going to shoot my Dad's old model 11 that day, her first ever with a 12 bore. When we soon spotted a loner headed our way I suggested she give it a try. If for no other reason, I thought, than to get the feel of the gun.

On a line that would take it past us at no more than 30 yards, and nearly the same height off the deck, the goose had its afterburners lit by the stiff 20-knot breeze on its tail. I watched over her shoulder as she tracked the bird, pulled ahead, and fired. Both she and the goose rocked hard, but the feathers she drew were from way too far back. "More lead, more lead!," I urged as Mary kept her head down and followed up with a second, but this time well-placed shot. The big bird balled up, its long neck folding backward as if in slow motion. Though its wind-driven momentum carried the goose a full 80 yards, I was on it like the eager pup I suppose I still was.

Mary killed another goose or two over the course of the next few years, but though she liked to tag along, (when it was warm enough), she gave up the shooting. Not because she didn't understand it, but because it just wasn't important to her.

I was convinced even then, that she'd be an understanding mother, to both our children and, hopefully, a succession of gundogs.

The geese that visited the Horicon continued to flourish. As they did their concentrations spread out from the marsh proper, to utilize roosting waters such as Green Lake and Puckaway to the west. Hunting opportunity was expanded proportionately. Those opting for the new West Central Zone out around the lake country would get four tags/year that could be used one/day. For three or four buddies working together, this added up to two or three weekends of quality gunning each season. By combining our resources our gang built a rig of over 20 dozen shell decoys that we effectively used to learn the pleasures of hunting field-feeding geese. No longer satisfied with pass shooting; we were intent on taking our birds over the spread, or not at all.

We enjoyed the scouting, the calling, the decoy placement, and even the time spent asking permission to hunt private ground. All of it made us better hunters. But more than anything, we enjoyed sharing our hunts with family and friends.

My Dad, Ken, and Dave's dad, Bob, had pretty much given up on waterfowling by that time. But we talked both out of retirement to sample a field hunt. We had done our homework and were set up on a hill-topped field near Markesan. There were nine of us total ... our biggest group ever ... laid out in a line along a heavily grassed fencerow that was shade-shrouded by the still standing corn at our backs to the east. In front of us, to our west, was our relatively massive spread of G&H shell decoys, enticingly visible on the short-clipped field of corn stubble.

Both Dave and I felt it was a perfect setup. That we ever totally agreed on anything was rare. That we did that day, was an omen.

The strung out band of geese materialized high over the woodlot in the section to our south. As they winged northward, with the ample chow in our stubblefield no doubt weighing heavily on their pea-brained minds, the birds lost altitude to the natural elevation. On they came, numbering more than 50 strong, in a ragged V-formation, and on a flight path that paralleled our line of gunners. With the geese no doubt keying on our blocks, all it took was our amateurish greeting call to turn them. As if they'd practiced their formation flying, the whole flock leaned on their left alerons and rolled to the right. On they came in a line confronting ours, coasting on tight-locked wings, gear down, and eerily silent.

My heart was pounding in my throat as I called the shot and all hell broke loose. The geese exploded into a clamoring, honking chorus as they clawed for air on their powerful wings, struggling to abort the landing. Guns spoke, and birds crumpled. Some crashed hard into the crisp-stalked standing corn. Others pounded the stubble with a resounding "splat." When the smoke cleared the nine of us had cleanly taken the same number of birds. It was our most spectacular volley ever.

Though there were high fives all around, the grins on Dad's and Bob's faces, as they needlessly thanked us, said it all. Though appreciated at the time, it wasn't until it was too late ... as Dave and I have learned in time ... that WE should have been thanking THEM.

Huntin' the Horicon came full circle for me in 1987, the year my oldest son, Billy, was first able to hunt. Ever since he began to show a serious interest in the outdoors as a youngster, it had been my dream that Billy, his Grandpa Kenny, and I would some day share a successful Horicon hunt. The icing on the cake would be seeing Shamus, my then fast-aging yellow dog ... the dog the boy had grown up with ... retrieve the lad's first goose.

With his intensive zone permit in hand, Billy, Gramps, the old dog, and I set out pre-dawn that mid-October Saturday. Our plan was to drive around the perimeter of the marsh, trying to find a good blind to rent for an afternoon hunt.

We were rolling west on highway 49 as it divides the heart of the federal refuge just at sunrise, and pulled over to enjoy that special show only a couple hundred thousand honkers can put on. As the swarms of rising geese blackened the clear blue sky Grandpa instructed Billy, "Look hard now. Look for the goose with your name on it."

"Let's hurry on. Let's go find us a blind," Gramps piped up, his sense of urgency bringing us back to reality.

And so we did. Turning south on a county road that roughly parallels the refuge line east of Waupun, we motored only a couple miles before pulling into a familiar farmyard, its driveway marked by an oversized goose silhouette advertising simply, "Blinds." I'd hunted there years before, and the landowner recognized me. Firmly grabbing my hand as only a dairyman can he urged, "Hurry on down to the fenceline blind east of the tracks. You know the one. The birds'll be comin' off good for a while yet. Stop by and settle up with me later."

Not believing our good fortune, we were outa' there in a cloud of dust. Only minutes later we were settling into the basic snow fence-ringed blind.

With geese already winging our way I instructed Billy to load up the long-barreled 1100. Even at that age the youngster was a capable shot. Short, but stocky and muscular, he'd fired a ton of target loads through the big autoloader that was nearly as long as Billy was tall. Though we hadn't talked about it, the 3-inch steel BBs, and their heavier recoil were a concern to both of us. I prayed for his success early on, knowing that a series of misses would not only shatter his psyche, but likely cause gun handling problems as well. Fortunately, it all proved a non-issue.

We hadn't been in the blind for more than five minutes when we spotted a trio of honkers coming head on, low enough for a shot. When I called it, Billy popped up, swung on the out-sized leader like he'd done it 1,000 times before, and yanked the trigger. The little guy rocked with the unfelt recoil and the goose shuddered, but kept pumping. Following up with a second blast before I could tell him to, the big goose locked its wings and banked left, falling out of formation on a dead-bird-glide that ended in a crash landing 70 yards out into the cattails. Looking at Shamus, I could see he had the mark. He made his typical short work of the retrieve, bounding through the thick, muck-bottomed cover with the enthusiasm of a pup; returning to deliver the bird, (as if he knew), right to Billy.

I looked at Dad. We looked at the boy/man. There were smiles all around. As there was, no doubt, from above. Billy's namesake, my Grandpa Bill Gordon Sr. was surely with us in spirit. Every bit as much as he had been with me for my first Horicon honker, more than 20 years earlier.

PART TWO

Expanding Our Horizon

*B*eing restless is a natural part of adolescence. But it's a condition that can be treated with the glorious acquisition of that first set of wheels. Wheels that open your world to adventure and misadventure alike. To good times, and almost inevitably, in the case of headstrong, testosterone-laced young lads, some fender-bending bad ones as well. And in that regard ... well ... we were no exception. But of all the newfound freedom that driver's license provided, nothing, (well, almost nothing, at least during daytime), seemed more practical than using it to expand our wildfowling horizons. To that end, we began to stray from our often over-crowded, but still beloved Marsh.

Now, as kids really, we were little more than wannabe members of the local, hardcore duck hunting community. My dad and uncle had given us a start and shown us the ropes as they knew them. But if we were going to go places, literally and figuratively in this world of wildfowling, it became obvious we'd be doing it on our own. So, with little more than hearsay to guide us, we rolled.

CHAPTER FOUR

Collins Remembers

Collins Marsh, in Manitowoc County, a state property developed primarily for waterfowl, was almost new at that time in my youth. And the word was it was providing consistent gunning, primarily on mallards, the likes of which the Sheboygan Marsh had never seen. We HAD to be part of the action. But other than being able, with the use of a road map, to find it, we didn't know where to begin! Not being the brightest bulbs in the box, common sense eventually prevailed. First we used our eyes to spot, not birds, but cars in the parking lots. Then we used our ears, listening for the direction of any gunfire. Following the sound, we used our legs and boundless energy to hike down the boot-worn footpaths of more-knowing hunters, in search of "the spots."

Some of these paths cut through cattail marshes that paralleled prominently posted, open water refuge areas. Others led deep into flooded woods, (legitimate flooded green timber as I'd came to learn later in life), that also bordered a block of refuge. The walks were long and arduous, particularly in the heavy, oversized rubber waders of the day. To get to the best spots, naturally, required traversing major stretches of boot-sucking, quicksand-like muck.

The highlight of hunting Collins was the abundance of birds. The newly flooded, primarily inaccessible wetland complex proved a major suckhole for ducks migrating through eastern Wisconsin. With shooting allowed pretty much on its fringes only, and little to no disturbance from boat traffic, the birds got real comfortable on the marsh.

The only drawback, we'd eventually realize, was that the vast majority of the hunting, or more accurately put, the shooting, was that of classic firing line. Whenever birds would cross "the line," high or low, they were sure to meet with a hail of gunfire. And as far as we were concerned at the time, that was the good news. All that mattered was that we were seeing more birds, and doing more shooting, than we ever had. Like the rest of the Collins hunters at the time ... firing line be damned ... we were happy hunters.

To hunt "the line" required little in the way of tactics. You had to either get up in the middle of the night to get a front row seat, (though even then it was likely to be standing room only), or you could arrive well after shooting time and wait for the frontliners to either fill up or leave in frustration after trying.

Whichever strategy you chose, hunting with a buddy or two was always a good idea. When dealing with numbers of hunters, we soon learned, there was strength and security in numbers of your own. Sad fact, but true.

In time ... in the span of only a couple years really ... though great weekday shooting could still be had when the flight was in and the weather "right," we soured on Collins. Competing with the ducks was fine. But physically competing with other hunters seemed, even then, not what our sport should be all about. Seeing way too much sky busting and greedy "claiming," we were outa' there.

But it wasn't without some fond memories. Not the least of which was hunting Collins all but two days of the skimpy 30-day duck season we had during my freshman year in college, and taking my then only one-allowed-mallard, on almost every outing.

When recalling those, and others of our earliest, best days at Collins, one of our group was always quick to mimic a DJ on the a.m. rock station we all tuned in. This personality, sporting the same last name as our Manitowoc County marsh, would introduce an oldie with the phrase, "Collins Remembers ... "

Well ... so do we!

CHAPTER FIVE

The Lure of the Big Lake

*L*ake *Michigan ... now ... that's where the ducks were! I'll surely never forget those childhood, late autumn, Sunday afternoon drives with Dad along county highway LS as it winds along the lakeshore between Sheboygan and Manitowoc. Whenever the lake came into view, most prominently at the Haven curve, its surface could be seen spattered with huge gumdrop-shaped flocks of fowl. Some rafts, surely numbering in the thousands of birds, rode the swell almost within gun range of the beach.*

And no one was hunting them!

Several years later, gazing out the window of my second floor homeroom at Sheboygan North one nasty November day, I marveled at the constant strings of ducks, fresh migrants no doubt, that the howling 'noreaster was blowing southward along the three or four block distant lakeshore.

And still, no one was hunting them!

"Someday. Somehow!" I vowed.

My first, futile attempts at hunting lake ducks were shorebound. A few of us similarly demented types would get together with all the decoys we had and find a spot along the beach near Haven or Hika. We'd wade as deep as we could given the surf conditions, to set a rig as elaborate as our budding imaginations would allow. Then we'd dig a forever-collapsing hole in the sand and brush it with available driftwood.

Still, when conditions were perfect, we scored a few divers, mostly 'bills and ever-gullible butterballs. When they weren't, as was usually the case,

the outings proved a lesson in futility. At best, the wind and waves would come up, first demolishing the spread, then washing it ashore as the surf overtook our blind. At worst, undertow would start to rip the rig out to sea, of which we'd invariably get an icy waderful as we struggled to pick up.

All early trials aside, we remained nothing if not enthusiastic. That enthusiasm eventually brought us to the conclusion that if we were ever going to be regularly successful on the big water, it would have to be from a boat. Heck, we were ALMOST adults by the time we figured it out.

My primary hunting partner at the time was buddy Dave Kovacic. We were quite the team, the two of us. Being the budding business planning, general manager-type; I planted the seed of the idea. Dave, the hulking truck driver was the General, (he had to feel he was in charge), AND the grunt in his one man, "Get outa' my way, I'll git'er done!," army. Fortunately, he was as stricken with the idea of big lake, open water hunting as I was. It was the fall of '68 when we set out to prove that we weren't, as some suggested, quite "right." That duck fever may have permanently impaired our judgement.

At the foundation of our effort was my wide-hulled, but only 14 foot long Alumacraft powered by a 20 horse Merc. It was a boat we felt plenty adequate early on, but which we'd come to learn, was far from it. Come early September we filled the boat with a rig of seven strings of diver decoys, each sporting 12 to 18 blocks, which we'd anchor with downrigger weights. Our simple blind consisted of a pair of smelt seines suspended on poles fit into the boat's rodholders.

Beginning with that first Saturday in October it was mud ducks and mud duck hunters, (as Dave had snidely come to call them), be damned. Come hell or high water, (the first, close, the second, a reality), we were committed, (or should have been).

We had our share of snafus early on to be sure, but we had some success right from the get go. Though more popular today, hardly anyone messed with the big water back then, and we were thrilled to find consistent, quality gunning. Sport that required little more than a boatride to have totally to ourselves.

Beginning that first year, and on through the next several, we enjoyed season-long gunning. Bluebills, truly abundant at the time, provided the bulk of the early season shooting. And given their aerobatic ability and fighter pilot mentality, they were by far the most pure fun.

But it was the scoters, ducks we really didn't know existed until that time, that often saved the day. The huge, glamorous white wings, and the slightly smaller, drab-colored common or black scoters, ultimately provided some of our most memorable moments. When it came to these seemingly ponderous, but deceptively fast and super tough targets, it was a matter of "no skill required." When we'd spot a line of these big, black ducks approaching, or just winging by, we quickly learned to stand up and wave our hats. Getting their attention, they'd often swing right in, or at least give us a close flyby, just as they did one glorious late October Saturday afternoon.

My good friend Joe Leibham had joined Dave and I that day. Not even close to being a serious waterfowler, Joe is a great, fun-loving guy. His good-natured company was always welcome, and his help in launching off the beach south of Sheboygan that day was greatly appreciated. We had no sooner put up the blind than Joe pointed and casually mentioned, "there's a bunch." It was a flock of scoters 12 birds strong. No need to flag, they had spotted our rig and winged our way. When the birds swung on their upwind turn they bunched up and came at us in a wad. When the smoke cleared only one bird had escaped.

"Aw geez. That's not good!" Joe muttered in mock disgust.

"Hey, what's wrong with that?" Dave replied defiantly as he gestured toward the bellied-up birds with his chest all puffed out.

Joe, knowing he had him, snickered and pointed out, "Hell, one more and we'd have rolled a strike!"

There were high fives all around.

It's fair to say that we pretty much fell in love with big lake hunting over the years. The quality of the hunt was special, but I'll be the first to admit that the quantity mattered. No matter what time of season, there was always something to shoot on Lake Michigan. And shooting ducks, after all, is a big part of hunting ducks, especially when you're young.

The variety of ducks, (virtually every specie of diver, save for harlequin and eider, visited our Lake Michigan rig at one time or another), kept things interesting as well. But never more so than late in the season. It was then that the oldsquaw was king.

There's really nothing in the world of a Wisconsin waterfowler that can compare with idling out of a Lake Michigan harbor under cover of darkness on a crisp, early winter day, then shutting the motor down to simply listen. Bobbing hypnotically on the rhythmic swells during false dawn, you're nearly overwhelmed by a gnawing feeling of personal insignificance in the face of all the natural majesty that surrounds you. Then you hear them. The eery, soul-stirring "oogah, oogah, ooooguh" calls of sqawducks resonating across the big lake's chilled surface. With enough light finally oozing across the horizon you spot the flight line. All religion and mystery aside, the hunt is on!

Hardly boat or blind shy, the challenge of oldsquaw hunting was rigging for the deeper, offshore waters they frequent. Once set up in their flightline, whether anchored or just drifting, you were in business. Given the longtailed duck's deceptive speed, 'squaws provided some of the toughest shooting we ever enjoyed.

Now, don't get the wrong idea. Our Lake Michigan hunting wasn't always a slam-dunk. Far from it.

From the point of our initial success on the big water, we rode a roller coaster of highs and lows not unlike the sometimes-mountainous crests and canyon deep troughs of its waves.

We surely dealt with our share of rough, hunt-ending, sometimes life-threatening weather. Some of it was expected. (Given an easterly blow, and knowing better, we'd give it a headstrong go anyway.) Some of it was unexpected. Like an unpredicted, gusting windshift finding us perilously distant from the harbor. In either case the result would be a wet ass at best, some tore up equipment, and the inevitable lecture by my Dad, (who still hovered protectively over us) at the landing, at worst.

As for dealing with cold weather ... well ... how do you really learn about frostbitten fingers or the effect of icing on a boat's stability, unless it's firsthand. And hypothermia? Hell, I'm not even sure it was a term back then. Drowning, or freezing to death we understood. But hypothermia?

When it comes to adventures with equipment, we had our share. It didn't take long to learn that substituting a shallow-draft, one-man marsh skiff for the stability of a truly built layout boat was not only impractical. It was suicidal! A rubber raft as a gunning platform seemed worth a try. But when a raft-mate lost his balance and blew a big hole in the water not a foot from the primary inflation chamber, while we were riding rollers in 60 feet of water, the idea quickly lost its luster.

For a while, launching my 14 footer off the beach with the help of my tough, new Blazer was the hot setup. But after sinking the boat on the first sandbar, thanks to the inevitable windshift-induced surf, on back-to-back outings, even WE began to have second thoughts. When we did it a third time and pulled the bow hook of the hull trying to drag the swamped craft ashore, then spent all afternoon repeatedly burying, digging, and winching out the THREE four-wheel drives it eventually took to retrieve the boat ... well ... consider it a costly lesson finally learned.

Still, looking back on them now, those big lake years were truly special. We thrilled then, to a type of hunting we still could today. But it's tough duty. One that takes a commitment, almost to the exclusion of all other waterfowl hunting, to make it work.

It was a commitment from which we eventually wavered.

CHAPTER SIX

Canada Calling

"Hey schoolboy," Dave's call began in his cocky, but friendly, challenging tone, "it's Canada calling!"

"Alright I'll bite. What the hell you talkin' about now?" I replied.

"Canada. Minnedosa, Manitoba. And ducks. All those dumb ducks the guys at the gun club have been blabbering about," Dave effused.

"Yeah, so what's your point?" I challenged.

"Let's go. Next week. Me and a couple of the guys are laid off next week. So let's go. Give 'em a shot!" he explained.

My head was spinnin'. It was my first semester down at the BIG school. And the next week was six-week exams! There was no way, especially given my heavy course load, that I could miss one, much less all of the big tests. I thought for a moment, but not much longer, knowing Dave was dead serious, then answered, "I'm in. Oh yeah, I'm in!"

It probably wasn't the smartest decision at the time, but it was one I never really regretted.

Dave, his dad Bob, who decided to join us at the last minute, and who provided the transportation in the form of his full-size Ford wagon, left Sheboygan about noon that Saturday. Our buddies, traveling in their souped up '55 Chevy left at daybreak. They couldn't wait. But they paid the price we'd come to find, in the form of not one, but two speeding tickets along the way.

After a straight-through drive, interrupted only by a two-hour roadside nap, we rolled into the Minnedosa area at daybreak. The sunrise soon illuminated what for us was a wonderful new world of rolling grainfields pock-marked with small blocks of aspen parklands, and a myriad of duck-splotched wet-lands. Whether it was a quarter acre roadside pond, a larger, rush-lined slough or lake, or just a patch of sheet water, the remnant of a recent downpour, all held waterfowl in varying species and concentrations.

It was as if we'd traveled through a time warp. In the span of less than a day's drive we'd transported ourselves to what appeared to be duck hunters' heaven.

We checked in at the local hotel, then crashed for a coupla' hours. Save for Bob, who easily could have, we were all too fired up to sleep. We had to get out on this no- hunting Sunday to further acquaint ourselves with the countryside and scout for a Monday morning hunt.

Predictably, Dave had different ideas about what looked good than I. His Dad sided with me, as we chose to hunt a field with several small sloughs and sheet water ponds holding a variety of puddlers. Dave led the rest of the guys to a long cattail-lined complex of lakes that they found covered with divers.

Bob and I had a wonderful time as we walked in that first morning, jumped a bunch of birds, then simply hunkered down in the skimpy cover to see what happened. The wonderfully happy, naive, obviously unpressured birds, soon began to trickle back, offering some classic, up close and personal shooting. When we left the field for the planned lunchtime rendezvous with the rest of the gang, it was with a near limit. Taking them as they came, we had a grand time gathering a mixed bag of gadwall, wigeon, mallard, and teal.

Dave was pretty happy with his group's success as well. Taking cover at a narrows that served us a pass between two large, lake-sized sloughs; the boys had done a ton of shooting, a lot more than their bag of 'bills, ring-necks, and redheads, should have required. But since shooting opportunity, not percentages was the issue, there were broad smiles all around.

As much as already making the trip an unqualified success, that first morning's hunt set the tone for the week. Though we enjoyed several group hunts, Bob and I, for the most part, went our own way, as did Dave and the rest of the guys.

Never hunting the same spot twice, we'd simply tool around spotting birds; then either jump shoot them, or flush them and pass shoot as they returned. The hunting was simple, easy, and productive. And besides, we didn't know any better. The joy of working the birds, and taking them over a well-set rig of decoys was not yet of paramount importance. Gunning and bagging birds was our priority. We were too early in our career to be concerned with how we were doing it. As long as it was legal, just doing it was all that really mattered.

The unexpected bonus on this trip proved to be Bob's company. A rifleman, deer hunter, camera buff, and pilot at heart, he had done very little duck hunting. His laid-back approach to the sport, as opposed to mine and Dave's at the time, had a lasting affect on me. Yeah, he seemed to enjoy the shooting well enough. But the perma-grin he wore all week was no doubt a result of his just "being there" in the outdoors, with the guys in general, and his son in particular, having a good time. Always willing to go with the flow, the only sense of urgency he exhibited had to do with cocktail hour. At the end of each hunting day he'd haul out his bottle of Metaxa and pour a hefty shot for he and I. Then, with the afternoon fast fading into evening, we'd salute our good fortune. It's a custom as fitting today as it was then.

As we hunted through that wonderful week we didn't encounter another hunter ... not one! One night I asked the hotel manager about the lack of hunting pressure.

"Oh, we see a few American hunters. But the locals don't bother much with ducks. We shoot the odd mallard, eh? Especially when the 'northerns' are in. But overall, it's fair to say we take the ducks for granted. We like the chickens and the geese, but most of that hunting is 40 to 50 miles east of here."

Well, we took the odd mallard too. But it was the gray ducks, brown ducks, and divers that kept us happily busy until that last glorious Friday. Dave, after encountering a few local upland enthusiasts in the pub, set his jaw, as he was wont to do, determined to give the chickens (a.k.a. sharptails), a go. And the rest of the troops sided with him. Bob and I were undecided.

Waking to find a fresh two-inch blanket of snow and a howling north wind, there was little question what I wanted to do. And Bob, not much of a hiker either, was more than willing to play along.

What we found at first light was a dull, wintry scene. Though the snow was fresh and spotless, the low, variously gray-shaded scud seemed determined to prevent the day from fully dawning.

But we soon found bright spots. Thousands of them. In the form of bright, greenheaded, orange-footed, northern mallards. Fresh in from who-knows-where, these colorful fowl lit up our world like so many bulbs on a Christmas tree.

As for the hunting they provided ... well ... we couldn't have had a better present. At our first stop Bob and I got out and walked over a rise in a barley field to find two dozen mallards, every one ass up, their big bright feet paddling air as they fed in the sheet water pond. We stood there a lot like a coupla' trapshooters ready to call, "pull," waiting for the birds to right themselves. Even for us, the gunning was high percentage.

Our hunt was over by mid-morning. But we spent the rest of the day cruising the suddenly wintry countryside, marveling at the birds and our surroundings. It was too bad, but the rest of our group missed the show, as they did the few chickens they encountered.

It sure was fun to see the look on Dave's face when he spotted our 16 fat, fully plumed greencaps draped across the Ford's front fender. I wish I knew what he was really thinking as he muttered. "Had a good day, huh?"

More than anything, I came away from this trip secure in the knowledge I'd been to a very special place. The fact that there had to be a lot of others just like it, set the table ... if hadn't been to that point ... in what would prove for me a lifetime of prairie-borne wildfowling adventure.

Inspite of my best sales efforts with the professors, I came back to 15 credits of "F." I never worked so hard in school as I did that semester just to pull off a "C" average. My parents were concerned with the lower-than-usual grades. But they got over it.

As a footnote ... Dave and I, along with my then very special friend Mary, returned to Minnedosa two years later. It was another spontaneous trip and another phenomenal hunt.

CHAPTER SEVEN

First Snows

*T*hough not bad, it was a disconcerting time in my life. My parents had always preached, "Go to school. Get a good job." So I did the first. But was having a tough time with the second.

I knew nothing about recession, a falling stock market, rising unemployment, and tough economic times. All of which were facts of life when I graduated college in '72. One thing I did know was that there were few challenging, entry-level positions available for a business school grad. Oh, I could have sold insurance. Or become a management trainee in a retail organization. But that wasn't the kind of "good" job I was after.

So, as I continued to mail resumes and apply for anything that looked interesting, I worked at a number of part time jobs that at least provided enough gas money to help support my hunting and fishing habit. One of those was that of a graveyard shift manager at a self-service gas station.

The bad news with this gig was that it gave me way too much time to dwell on my situation. Sitting there at three in the morning, contemplating in which direction the next turn in my life would take me, almost became an obsession.

The good news was that the job gave me mornings off to chase critters and clear my mind. And that's just what I decided to do that day in late October.

Cruising the lakeshore at daybreak, I was looking for migrating geese moving inland from their Lake Michigan roost. Just past the Cleveland swamp near Hika Bay I happened to glance westward, noticing several out-of-place white spots in the harvested cornfield. Pulling over to get a better look with the binocs, I couldn't believe my eyes. The "spots" were four ma-

ture snow geese happily grubbing away. I'd been looking for the far more common Canadas, but was thrilled to find the ever-rare-in-our-flyway snows. To that point in my life I'd never had a crack at those mysterious, majestic arctic geese.

After studying them for a few minutes I determined the birds were feeding toward the field's eastern fenceline. Hastily ... before someone else spotted them ... I planned a stalk. Easily able to walk to the swamp unseen, I'd then have to carefully pick my way through the cedars on the south end of the cornfield. From there it would be a belly crawl up the fenceline.

All went well until the brushy cover along the fence gave out. From a prone position I peeked through the last tuft of grass, marked the birds as best I could, and made my move. Once on my knees I knew I'd blown it. The birds, the four snows and a solitary eagle-headed blue I hadn't previously noticed, were just too far. As they jumped I shouldered Dad's old Remington but didn't send any of the #4 lead loads I'd stuffed it with down the barrel.

Totally deflated, it was then that I first felt the cold. My well-worn jeans and light windbreaker hadn't been up to the task of keeping my skin separated from the icy muck and slime. With the adrenaline rush subsiding, a full body shiver took over.

But then a strange thing happened. The geese, which I'd helplessly watched wing back out over the lake, were coming back. After a single, low pass, they cupped hard, confidently touching down in the center of the stubblefield. Either the allure of the abundant waste grain was overwhelming, or they judged that strange, mud-covered, bear-like form to be not so threatening afterall. "Or maybe," I pondered, "could it be destiny?"

Whatever, I watched hopefully as the geese started to work toward the western fenceline this time. So it was mud-be-damned as I slithered back down my fence, stumbled through the cedars once more, then started up the west fence on all fours. I made good time given the much taller cover, occasionally stopping to verify the birds' location.

Taking a final peek I put them directly out from one oddly tilted fence post. "If I can make it to that point," I promised myself, "I'll spring my trap."

It was then that I noticed him. Another hunter creeping down the fence from the north. It was obvious however, that he didn't see me.

Putting it in high gear I made it to my fence post. And when I parted a clump of weeds at its base I found myself eye-to-eye with one very startled snow goose. The geese were already airborne as I came to my knees agunin'.

If ever the Red Gods smiled on me, it was then. My eyes focused on that nearest snow and when the gun spoke "two" birds buckled up tight, not 25 yards out. In a dreamlike sequence I swung hard left, clobbering a third at

35 yards or so; then pushed the Weaver-choked barrel back to the right in a hope-and-poke effort, scratching down the fourth snow with a barely broken wing tip at 50 plus. As I hustled after the cripple the disoriented blue circled well within range of his fallen buddies not once, but three times! I could easily have taken it out, filling my five bird limit. But I quite consciously didn't.

I can't explain why, but it felt "right" to see that goose finally sail away, fully lit by the sun and in brilliant contrast to the clear, bluest of blue skies. Just as with mine, I wondered what lay ahead for it in the bird's far-wandering life.

It was then that I once again became aware of my competition. Standing there, 80 yards short of the action, and clearly as wet and muddy as me, I motioned the hunter over. As he clumsily, shyly shuffled up to me in obviously oversized galoshes, wearing a tattered wool jacket layered over patched bib overalls, and carrying a rusty old single shot hammergun; I correctly guessed he was a local farmboy, barely 14 or 15 years old, on a preschool outing. There was no doubt he'd worked as hard as I had trying to sneak those geese. And the disappointment that showed in his eyes, even through the severely cracked left lens of his wire-rimmed glasses, had laid him as low as I was high.

"Here ... take one of these birds," I offered, holding out a prime white specimen.

"Naw! You're kidding, right?" he softly replied. Then he thought for a moment and piped up "But geez ... you know ... my mom would sure like one."

Stuffing the bird's heavily feathered neck into the lad's scrawny, mud-caked hand I emphasized, "It's your bird. You earned it."

At that he slung the goose over his shoulder and strode off, stopping after only a few steps to turn back and end our brief conversation with an appropriately simple but heartfelt, "Thanks mister!"

I had to chuckle. To that point in my life, no one had ever called me "Mister." Little did I know it was the forbearer of things to come.

As I turned to slog my way back to the old Pontiac, feeling the soothing warmth of the morning's sun on my back for the first time that day, the words of a John Denver ballad, "Sunshine, on my shoulder, makes me happy," came to mind.

"Yeah it does," I thought, "but not nearly as much as does the heft of those First Snows in my hand."

There was no doubt I was happy. But for some reason I felt relieved as well. I really understood, for the first time, that with patience, hard work, and the support of family and friends, "things" in this sometimes-difficult life, eventually could and do work out.

PART THREE

The Shape of Things to Come

*A*s a product, in great part, of the live-for-today '60s, I hadn't taken much in life to that point, very seriously. But then I met that "someone special" and everything changed. I suppose nagging maturity had been creeping in right along, but having Mary in my life hastened the process.

When I finally got grounded in a decent job, the next logical step was marriage. And so we set out on what has been a wonderful voyage together. Our long term success no doubt due to having our priorities straight right from the start.

To this day, it's always been family, work, and other interests, in that order. The balance of all three being critical.

The outdoors in general and wildfowling in particular had always been a big part of my life; and so it became part of Mary's. At times her interest being active. And at others, more passive. Still, it remains today the glue that's kept us together as we continue to travel life's highways and byways. A journey that began in earnest on our 1974 honeymoon.

CHAPTER EIGHT

The Honeymoon

We were married in August '74, but we opted to postpone our honeymoon until the first two weeks in October. It was then we planned a trip to Luseland, Saskatchewan. My stated goal was to hunt specklebellies for the first time. Mary's was pure adventure. We'd find plenty of both.

I'd gotten the idea from an old shooting buddy, Ari DeZeeuw. After a couple rounds of Saturday afternoon skeet it was his practice to enjoy a few more of brandy and beers. During which the stories of his many years of waterfowling would begin to flow. Though all attention-getters, none of his tales were more enchanting than those of his travels to Luseland; where he'd chase ducks and geese on the area's sprawling wheat fields and abundant wetlands.

I (we) had to go.

Like Sonny and Cher's tune said, we didn't have the proverbial "pot" at the time. Mary, in her secretarial job, was making as much as I was, and that wasn't much at all. We lived in the low rent upper flat of her grandparent's house. And a savings account seemed a distant goal. Still, we scraped enough dough together for a down payment on a brand new Blazer, (the hottest set of wheels there was at the time), loaded it with the bare essentials, including three dozen venerable, cardboard and paper mache G&H Canada goose shell decoys I got off Ari, and set off west by norwest one gorgeous late September morning.

After a long first day's haul to Minot, the afternoon of day two, October 1, found us heading north out of Moose Jaw into a raging blizzard. By the time we'd four-wheeled to Saskatoon there was a good 10 inches on the level and four-foot drifts in the ditches. It wasn't pretty. We holed up that night in a motel in Saskatoon, a city we found transformed into a ghost town as we searched out a restaurant. Turned out the snow wasn't the problem. It was game one of the first ever Canada/Russia hockey series that had every Canadian glued to his or her TV.

The next day dawned clear and 17 degrees cold. The countryside appearing Siberian in every sense. A lot of the smaller potholes we passed were frozen solid. Others held pods of ducks huddled in their centers, furiously paddling to keep the water open. Things looked bleak and I was concerned, but no more than we were committed. So we rolled on.

We made Luseland, a tiny, little-more-than-crossroads western Saskatchewan town fast by the Alberta Border, just at dusk. It wasn't hard to find the Royal George Hotel, the berg's only lodging. A classically old structure, with a bar and dining on the main floor, full service rooms on the second, and a dormitory setup on the third. Thanks to my inadequate planning, we were relegated to the exclusively hunter-occupied third floor. The rooms were ... well ... quaint and clean. But having to first clear the community bathroom, then guard it like a hallway monitor when Mary needed to use the facilities, was an interesting task. Though good-natured, I got my share of grief for having a woman on the floor.

Our first full day in the Luseland area dawned sunny and snow-melting warm, pushing well into the 60s by noon. While up to the challenge, what had been our shiny new truck quickly took the muddy, grimy appearance of a venerable hunting buggy. One that sure wasn't too pretty to be approaching landowners with when asking permission to hunt.

And, after locating a stubblefield full of specks late that afternoon, that's just what we were hoping to secure as we pulled into the Bergin family farmyard. Before I could knock on the door it popped open, and Lori stepped out promptly offering me his hand. After making introductions and after a few minutes of the usual small talk, I got around to the obvious. Lori was noticeably uncomfortable, and kicked the dirt a bit, explaining that he'd promised to hunt with his wife's grandfather the next morning. Still without saying "no" outright, he invited Mary and I in to meet his wife and "Grandpa Joe."

The oldtimer was pretty standoffish, but Lori's wife was a sweetheart, and thanks to a rye and water or two, the conversation, given that we found out we were the same age, soon resembled that of old friends.

Blazers were not yet available in Canada at the time, and when Lori remarked about it, I flipped him the keys and offered, "Go take 'er for a spin." He responded with, "Yeah. OK. Let's take it for a run around the ranch."

We saw plenty of birds on our late afternoon tour. And when I remarked how comfortable the wheatfield grazing specklebellies appeared, no doubt all but drooling out the window, he finally caved in.

"Aw heck. Why don't you guys come hunt with us in the morning? Old Joe might be a little upset, but he'll get over it."

I, for one, hardly slept that night. But getting Mary suited up and out the door at 5 a.m. was a bit of a chore.

Arriving at the wheatfield as only the slightest sliver of predawn light sliced the prairie apart from the starlit sky, we found Lori and old Joe sippin' coffee in the cab of their truck.

Our setup was as basic as basic could be. For cover we set three blinds constructed of the small 14 or 15 inch high bales that were scattered about the field. One-man blinds each for Joe and Lori, and a slightly larger one for Mary and I to share. The plan was to hunt from our knees, simply hunching over and huddling tight to the straw when we had birds in the air. Among the blinds we scattered my three dozen shells and a dozen of his rough-cut silhouettes Joe insisted we add. There'd be three shooters. Though she'd killed a few honkers back home, pulling the trigger was nothing if not totally unimportant to Mary, by that time.

As shooting time arrived I took a mental picture of my wife that I still have today. Dressed in all the warm clothes she had, camoed with a poncho-cut piece of smelt seine, and topped by a Jones-style cap with the brim turned down all around, she was quite the fancy-looking bride.

Our first birds came as a trio, scraping low over the field from the roost pond just over a half mile distant. Totally oblivious to our presence, they were obviously intent on having breakfast where they had, as Lori explained, for the past week. The three amigos spotted our decoys and sucked to them like they were their long lost buddies.

Seeing they were coming from his side, I waited for Joe to cut loose, which he promptly did, his ancient A-5 spitting lead faster than I thought it could. But nothing fell until I made my move, stoning; (at least I thought I did), the leader. When Joe popped up, walked out and grabbed "his" bird ... MY first specklebelly ever ... , I wasn't going to argue.

Knowing how I could be, Mary jabbed me in the side and with a grin told me, "Be nice now!"

The next flight was a half dozen birds strong but they blew us off at the last second. Lori managed to scratch down tail-end Charley as they were on the way out. Though I didn't see or hear him shoot, old Joe promptly picked up the second bird of his two-speck limit. I looked at Lori. He only shrugged his shoulders and grinned.

The next two bunches worked perfectly, and our hunt was over well before breakfast. I was elated with my first specks, and admittedly more confused than amused by old Joe's behavior. Lori explained later that Joe was not only nearly deaf, his eyesight was fast-failing as well. A combination that made him ill at ease around people, especially strangers. He wasn't totally shy though, being more than willing to take center stage in a hero-type photo I set up back at the ranch.

After an instant replay on the specks the next morning, Mary and I spent the better part of the week travelling and enjoying the game-rich countryside amid a comfortable spell of Indian summer weather, taking a duck or two when I had the chance. And we had some pleasant hikes in pursuit of the occasional flock of Huns we'd invariably flush from the roadside. But perhaps our most memorable hunt came one cool, breezy, sun-splashed afternoon.

It was already getting late when we came upon a freshly swathed barley field literally infested with ducks. The only sign of human life in the area was a cluster of buildings, and graineries a mile distant. Even at first glance, the small, faded gray farmhouse struck me as unusually quaint. Rapping on the door I was surprised, though I shouldn't have been, to find a middle-aged woman dressed in full Hutterite fashion, greet me. She promptly invited me into her kitchen, lit only by two long, dust-clouded, laser beam-like shafts of light streaming through its windows.

"Sure you can hunt. Please do. It'll help save our crop," she quietly, almost shyly replied to my request. Then she asked, "Would you and your wife like to come in for some cookies and milk?" Without consulting Mary, who probably would have, I politely declined. I felt bad about it, but getting on with the hunt was my top priority.

We hurried out to the field then, flushing hundreds ... no ... probably thousands of ducks, primarily mallards, but a sprinkling of pintails as well, as we advanced. After tucking into the thick, high-fluffed rows of swath we laid back, totally concealed, and waited. But not for long.

In minutes clouds of birds began streaming back to the field, some dropping on tightly cupped wings and without any hesitation, right into our laps. It was a matter of sensory overload. Alerted to their imminent appearance by the roar of air ripping through their pinions, we'd look up to find a sea of orange feet, backlit by flashing, silvery underwings, closing in on us like the headlights of an oncoming truck in a 3D movie. Then ... if I didn't shoot, and after a final face-washing rush and gush of air ... there they'd be, walking, gabbling, and chattering all around us.

The shooting, when I so chose, was a slam dunk. Employing my 1100 skeet gun on targets 20 yards and under proved the hot set up. And in only minutes I had eight prime greencaps on the stubble. Dogless at the time, Mary did the retrieving. I still kid her today about how cute she looked with those ducks in her mouth.

Like draining every last drop from a fine bottle of wine, we lingered, and thrilled to the spectacle until last light. Not unlike a scene from Hitchcock's "The Birds," we still had ducks whirling and landing all around us. And we quite literally kept kicking them off the swath as we walked out of the field with the northern lights beginning to strobe in the star-filled night sky.

It was an amazing experience. To this day ... at least as far as ducks are concerned ... I've never seen anything quite like it.

Stopping back at the then lantern-lit farmstead, the lady of the house was glad for the birds I offered her. Incredibly she couldn't THANK US enough for hunting.

We couldn't believe our good fortune.

And so our time in Saskatchewan came ... as all good things must ... to an end. It was ... thanks primarily to the special people we met ... a mission accomplished.

PART FOUR

The NoDak Years

*H*aving scheduled the time, we spent a couple days touring North Dakota and visiting a number of that state's National Wildlife Refuges on the road home from Luseland. Never having spent any time in the Roughrider State before, we were, to say the least, impressed. Not only with the sprawling, wetland-laced prairie and the fact that there were waterfowl everywhere; but that, no matter how many side roads we intentionally traveled, there wasn't a hunter to be found! It was a situation I vowed to investigate further, if for no other reason than North Dakota was much closer to home. Hunting there could better fit my needs in that family growing, career-expanding time of my life.

CHAPTER NINE

Let's Go Joe

The more I researched it the more fired up I got about NoDak. But there were a few obstacles to overcome before I could plan that first adventure.

First off, I'd have to get permission from "Mom." Mary, my most recent running mate, was with child and due in late summer. Though she knew she'd have her hands full with that first little duck hunter-to-be; she understood my need even then, (as she would for the rest of our lives), and with a motherly sigh, relented.

That hurdle cleared, I'd have to find a new hunting partner. Dave was the most logical choice, but he was working construction and couldn't get off. So I talked to Joe about a "road trip." Explaining that I needed to break in that year's new Blazer, and that a lot of off-roading would likely be involved, piqued his interest. Realistically, he could take or leave the hunting. But mention an all around good time, especially one involving a steering wheel, and he was up for that!

My plan came together when I read of an outfitter operating out of Rock Lake, North Dakota. I phoned him, checked his references, and booked a three-day, guided hunt for Joe and I. The package was a little spendy, especially at that time of my life, but I hoped it would be educational enough to send me on my freelancing way. It was. And in some very unexpected ways.

I'd never been on a guided hunt before and was more than a little uncomfortable at the prospect of being a "sport," and having someone looking over my shooting shoulder. Making matters worse was the fact that we were the youngest clients in camp by at least 20 years. Oh, everyone was friendly enough, but it was apparent the other hunters, repeat customers every one, were far more affluent and seasoned than we were. That we were newbies was awkward. That we weren't obviously big spenders, (or

likely heavy tippers), seemed to put us at a disadvantage.

Still, I couldn't say our guide didn't try. We set snow goose spreads, learning full well of the effort that takes, each of the three mornings we were there. But the shooting they produced was poor. Each day, just after shooting time, we'd get a crack at a flock or two of the frustratingly high-kiting snows. But the gunning was far rangier than any we'd ever experienced. There was no doubt Joe and I didn't have the sight picture those 50- to 60- yard, and sometimes longer shots our guide, often to our total surprise, called, as he came up blazing away. And our three-inch deuces, compared to the marvelously lethal four buck he shot, didn't seem up to the task either.

Given the pleasant, calm, sunny, early autumn weather, the morning goose flights petered out pretty quickly. After they did we'd spend the rest of the time, until the 1 p.m. closure, getting acquainted with the basic futility of trying to creep feeding flocks. Though more failed than not, our orchestrated attempts at ambush did produce a handful of birds, including a triple-banded blue, that the Fish and Wildlife Service informed me was three years old, and which still graces my man-cave's wall today.

Now, we were told there were "only" an estimated 5,000 snows and blues in the area at the time of our hunt. Not enough, our guide said, to provide top notch gunning, Still, that seemed like an awful lot to me, especially as I marveled at their seemingly endless return-to-roost flights each evening. Passing over Rock Lake, jagged, undulating lines of these boisterous birds etched the prairie sky like so many cracks in a shattered pane of glass. It was a spectacle unlike any I'd ever seen. I thrilled to it then. And though I've been fortunate enough to have witnessed it countless times since, I still thrill to it today.

Though it lit a fire in me, sending me down what would be a lifelong road of adventure; in terms of birds in the bag, my first real introduction to the white geese and their uniquely wild ways, was not highly productive.

Our afternoon duck hunts were another matter.

The abundant sloughs and potholes nearby Rock Lake all held ducks by the dozens, and sometimes, thousands. And our guide put us on the best of them. Casually driving up to a hole holding what he judged to be enough birds for a good shoot, we'd flush them, throw a small rig of decoys, then simply hunker down in the tulies and await their return. Once it started, the shooting, if not fast and furious, was at least always steady. And unlike the tall geese, we shot well on the ducks in that situation we were far more accustomed to.

More than just duck hunting, (which was really mallard shooting, since our guide pretty much insisted we work on the "big" birds only); it was the enthusiastic work of his dog that made those hunts special.

A smallish, barly straw colored female golden, Brandy would begin to quiver at the sight of approaching birds, then moan ever-so-soulfully until she was sent for the retrieve. It was her pure, live-for-the-moment enthusiasm that made me tell Joe, "That's it. I gotta' have a dog like that someday."

After our intense three-day initiation into the world of North Dakota 'fowling, we headed west to burn the rest of our week. Stopping in the Bottineau area for a couple days, and thanks to a tip from a friendly soul in the local café, we found our way to "the River," as the locals called it, but which is by name, the J. Clark Salyer NWR.

We had been duly impressed by the number of geese in the Rock Lake area. But the tens of thousands that poured off the river as we watched and scouted that first day was mind-boggling.

The next darker-than-dark, fog-bound morning found us stumbling along the refuge fence toward the indescribable racket of Lord-knows-how-many snows on the roost. As we waited, breathing as hard from sheer excitement as the mile-long hike, and with dim daylight finally soaking through the gloom, the river pool below us exploded in a thunderous roar. It was unlike anything we'd ever heard.

The geese came at us in unseen waves. We could hear the thick air being crushed by powerful wings, even amid all their raucous barking, as flight after flight passed over, but out of sight. Then suddenly, with the onset of more daylight, the odd flock would materialize, fuzzy gray/white silhouettes against a blindingly white background, 30 or 40 yards overhead. When quick enough, we snapped off a round or two. If lucky, a bird would tumble, sometimes smacking the wheat stubble in sight. Others, thudded to earth within earshot, but somewhere out in the haze. All in all it was a surreal experience.

We were still laying in the taller grassy cover along the fence line, with the fog finally having burned off, when I spotted a pickup slowly rolling along the edge of a standing sunflower field just to our west. The truck would stop every couple hundred yards, and after a muffled "pop, pop" a cloud of black-birds would lift and wheel from the 'flowers. When the driver spotted us he made an abrupt turn and headed our way across the stubblefield.

"Spose we're in trouble now," Joe moaned.

"Shouldn't be," I countered. "Nothing here was posted."

Turned out we weren't.

The man behind the wheel, a young farmer about our age, stuck his head out the window, and with an ice-breaking smile introduced himself as he extended his hand in classic prairie-folk fashion.

"Hi guys. I'm Lynn Schepp, the landowner hereabouts. Hope I didn't ruin your hunt. I was just flingin' a little lead at the darn black birds, tryin' to keep 'em outa' my crop."

We introduced ourselves in turn, explaining that our hunt was over anyway. Lynn offered us a ride back to our truck, which we gladly accepted. Taking him up on his friendly offer, we then followed him to his house where we were invited in for coffee. We left little more than an hour later, not only as friends, but with an open invitation to "come back and hunt anytime." (It was an invitation I've been taking Lynn up on for nearly 30 years now.)

"Only on the prairie!" Joe offered, shaking his head as we drove off.

With only a couple days left to kill, we motored west of Minot, out to the countryside around Ross and Stanley. What we found was a piece of a prairie duck hunter's heaven. From large, permanent lakes to small, shallow potholes and sheetwater ponds, all of which held fowl, a water hunter's options were unlimited. (At the time we had no clue as to the wonders of dryland hunting for ducks.) There were no posted signs. And we didn't see or hear another hunter. Without being selective, just taking them as they came, we happily, almost casually, gunned 12 species, a combination of divers and puddlers, in a day and a half's worth of hunting.

We were running late, trying to squeeze every last minute out of the adventure, and had to make a straight-through power drive home. But we'd been successful. Not just in the hunt, but in sampling the smorgasbord of wildfowling opportunity NoDak had to offer. It's a menu from which we continue to dine today.

CHAPTER TEN

New Blood

*T*wisting his arm, I convinced Joe to tag along on one last, for him, career-ending expedition the following year. His priorities were changing, and waterfowling just didn't rank high among them. So it seemed timely to bring in some new blood. Which I did in the form of a youngster nearly a generation younger than me, by the name of Steve Hiebing.

I first met Steve in the Sheboygan Harbor during a duck season years earlier. He and his two same-minded buddies, all no more than 14 years old at the time, would manually push their way- too- small and unreliably powered duck rig, on a four wheel dolly, the one city block from his parent's house to the harbor boat ramp. With only a rag tag rig of decoys, consisting primarily of black and white painted bleach bottles, they were limited from a practical and safety standpoint, to hunting along the breakwall inside the outer harbor. Often hunting just outside the harbor, Dave and I would kind of keep an eye on the "kids," as we pretty accurately called them, just in case they got into trouble. One breezy Sunday morning we chased down a couple of their cripples, unbeknownst to them, on the open water. Pretty much making their day, we handed the plump pair of 'bills over to them later at the ramp. Not unlike most youngsters, (been there, done that), they shot a lot and bagged very little. That they were out there, like us, every chance they got impressed me to no end. I suppose in Steve and his gang, I saw more than a little of myself those few short years earlier.

By the time he was out of high school Steve was a regular at the local gun club. I always enjoyed shooting with him. It was a chance to get to know him better.

At that time Steve was a quiet, strong, wiry, strait-laced young man. Though already a talented carpenter, he was, even then, a diehard, fully committed waterfowler first and foremost. Into gun- stock making, layout boat building, and restoration of old double guns long before it was fashionable, the only romance in Steve's life at the time was the outdoors in general, and anything to do with wa- terfowl in particular. For the most part, and for what it was worth, he was my kinda' guy. And when I offered, he jumped at the chance to join us in NoDak. We welcomed his energy and enthusiasm.

Joe, Steve, and I enjoyed some pretty decent snow geese shoots on that trip. Hunting mainly on or near the Schepp farm with my eight dozen new shell decoys, supplemented by a hundred rags-on- a-stick that Steve had hastily fashioned after a little research, we were able to throw a pretty decent rig. One from which we were thrilled to kill a half dozen or so snows each day. But the fact that other hunters, obviously more experienced and with more elabo- rate spreads, were doing much better, was not lost on us.

By the end of the week we realized we'd have to step it up a notch the next season, especially given the burgeoning number of goose hunters in the area and the competition they provided. But Steve was into it. And that was a good thing.

Snow geese, by that time, had become number one in my wild- fowling world. I was absolutely stricken by their striking beauty and uniquely wild nature then, and I remain evermore so today. Given my druthers, I'd have been happy to hunt the white geese in the mornings and simply watch, scout, and photograph them in the afternoons. But it had been my tales of the fabulous duck hunting that, more than anything I realized later, lit Steve's fire. So we spent our afternoons running and gunning the pothole country well over 100 miles, and a two hour one-way drive west of the Clark Salyer.

It made for some long days, but the sheer number of ducks, the total absence of posted land, and the apparent non-existence of competing hunters back in those years (the '70s and early '80s)

made for some world-class, multi-species hunts.

I'll admit I almost ... ALMOST ... took those duck hunts for granted. Their only drawback was that in Steve, they created a monster of sorts.

Being a product of a goose-deprived youth, and thrilling to the abundant opportunity NoDak provided, I certainly had geese on the brain. Steve grew up with the explosion of goose hunting opportunity in Wisconsin, but sadly, with the deteriorating quality of the duck hunting in our local area. When he found in NoDak the type of sport written about in his prized collection of books detailing and glamorizing the good old days, the "golden era" of waterfowling, Steve rightfully thought he'd died and gone to heaven. So it's fair to say that while our interests were basically the same, (ie. the quest for quality waterfowling), the stage was set for some goose hunter vs. duck hunt conflict.

Like any reasonable men agreeing to disagree, it was quite the balancing act we orchestrated over the next several years when first Steve's best buddy, John Butzen, then eventually their third musketeer, Clete Leonhard, joined in our by-then-traditional North Dakota adventures. I was fast into becoming a big sky, field-oriented snow *goose addict. Willing to go to bigger guns and loads, and do the long-range gunning commonly required, I found myself in the minority. Sticking stubbornly to their 2 ¾ inch guns, and birds-in-your-face-or-not-at-all, purist's philosophy, often put the boys and I at odds. Still, thanks in great part to their substantial effort, ingenuity, and patience (with me), we got a lot more proficient in our pursuit of the white goose. When conditions were "right," (ie. we lucked into the peak migration, there was an abundance of juveniles in the flock, and the weather, in terms of wind and low ceilings was with us), we enjoyed our share of near-limit shoots. Though tough to do, I had to bite my tongue and go with the majority flow when, even on days with birds still decoying, we had to pull the pin on the goose hunt and head for the duck-laden hills.*

Even when scouting for a duck hunt, we had our moments. I'd commonly insist on motoring past slough after duck-holding slough, all of which could probably have provided a decent shoot, until we found a "mother load." The old man (me) would try the lads' patience, but even Steve by then, knew from experience that it could be worth it.

When all said and done, I was as thrilled as any of the boys by the many great duck hunts, admittedly thanks to their insistence, we shared. Certainly "the" most memorable was that first day at "the pass."

CHAPTER ELEVEN

The Pass

It had been a great week. The goose hunting had been the best we'd seen yet, and the ducking, primarily for puddlers, had been almost too slam-dunk easy. Topping it all off for me was the performance of my first, and then only 1-year-old Lab, Shamus. The big yellow dog, just under 90 pounds of muscle and sinew, had come of age, retrieving well over 160 birds for us those first five days of the trip.

But then, come Thursday night, Mother Nature dealt us a heavy blow in the form of a howling prairie blizzard. Dumping 12 inches on the level, but filling the roadside ditches to field level, we awoke that Friday in early October to still-gusting winds and a premature winter wonderland. The best we could do with the geese was huddle up to a utility pole and try some impossible pass shooting as they blew off the refuge in waves, with more hospitable, southerly climes on their birdy minds.

Though the driving was treacherous, even I quickly agreed that it would be ducks or bust that day. Out west of Kenmare, slowly four-wheeling along a barely passable back road we'd never traveled before, we topped a rise only to promptly skid to a halt, barely able to grasp our good fortune. There before us spread two sloughs ... well, one small lake actually, and a pothole a quarter of its size ... nearly, but not quite totally separated by a cat-tail-lined peninsula. The frothing, chopping surface of both bodies of water were speckled with bobbing black and white ducks. But wadded tightly up against, and in the lee of the peninsula was an exclamation point-shaped raft of bluebills numbering at least in the hundreds, maybe even a thousand birds, from which stragglers constantly took wing and into which others landed, as they traded over that finger of land, that "pass."

It wasn't much of a plan really, After rushing out onto the pass we simply hunkered down in the 'tails. There we waited, without anyone saying it, for someone to take the first poke; knowing that when they did all hell would break loose.

Steve's venerable old double-barreled Baker, the Batavia Leader, finally broke the ice, quite literally, as he splashed a nice blackhead from a strafing flock into the offshore slush the big lake was making. Crunching through the shore bound shell ice, Shamus handled the hard, and hardening water ... the first he'd ever seen ... as if it wasn't even there.

At Steve's shot our world came alive with bluebills. Swirling all around us, some high, some on the deck, and others everywhere in between, jetting through the crisp air like the fighter pilots of the duck world they truly are, our gun barrels warmed to the task at hand.

The action was frenetic. And in the battle of the 'bills, it was every man for himself. Not waiting for "candy birds" we took our shots as they came, up and downwind alike. There was a lot of hooting and hollering. And a lot of missing. Still, there were birds tumbling everywhere, falling into the deep snow on land, splashing into the water on both sides of the pass, and crashing into the tulies. Shamus was on cruise control, snapping up every fall he marked. Those he didn't or couldn't, we broke from the shooting to help him with. Though we had to swat a couple hard-diving cripples, we didn't lose a bird.

There was no doubt these were fresh, yet-to-be hunted birds. And inspite all of the commotion, they kept buzzing, in true kamikaze fashion, what were some apparently food-rich waters.

It was a dreamlike hunt. One that was over as quickly as it had started. I wish I had a picture of the yellow dog lying, huffing and puffing in the snow, his ice-tipped coat casting a halo-like aura when suddenly backlit by the late afternoon sun poking through the wintry overcast. Wearing a goofy, shit-eating grin he proudly guarded that pile ... his pile ... of 'bills. But then I suppose I do have that special image in my mind's eye. I wrote these words based on it afterall.

To this day, whenever we get together to reminisce, the story of that unbelievable diver hunt at The Pass is one of the first told.

CHAPTER TWELVE

Starting Over...
Again

*T*he boys and I had a good run, enjoying our annual excursions
to North Dakota well into the '80s. Though we occasionally had
added company, (Dave Warnke or Bob Burton), for the most part
it had remained the four of us. But as they always do, times were
changing. A major drought had settled onto the prairies and we
were first-hand witnesses to the associated, dramatic decrease in
ducks. Even more alarming was the obvious degradation of habitat. We were shocked to see many of the potholes and sloughs we'd
hunted for years not only dry up, but many of them tiled, plowed,
and planted. Whole sections of wetlands were lost, apparently forever. While these changes were sobering, so too was their evolving
lifestyle as the boys, one by one, succumbed to marriage and its
challenging array of new responsibilities. Dakota waterfowling
was something they couldn't see their way clear to continuing, at
least at that time in their family building lives.

So I found myself at a crossroads once again. As we grew older
many of my cronies ... Dave, Joe, and others ... many who had been
as enamored with wildfowling as I early on, fell by the wayside.
The points system, steel shot, ever-more elaborate waterfowl regu-
lations in general, and the distraction and glamour of big game
hunting all caused a decline in the number of waterfowlers from
mine and the immediately preceding generation. Still, I persisted.
Though I enjoyed and was interested in virtually everything the
outdoors had to offer, from day one with my Dad and uncle, I knew
that waterfowl and waterfowl hunting would remain at the top of

the list for the rest of my life. Though I've traveled down my share of sporting side roads, I'm glad to say I've never doubted or regretted my conviction.

Now, a key component of our grand sport is who we pursue it with. And teamwork, in the world of wildfowl, usually keys our success. I was acutely aware of that as I made my fall's plans in '88. Though I'd tried my best, I couldn't find any new candidates to join up for the NoDak hunt. Given that our Canada goose hunting in eastern Wisconsin was pretty darn good, even I contemplated staying home that year. But not for long. I'd go solo if need be. Knowing there was no way Shamus and I could mount an all out assault on our own, I was confident the experience would still be worth the effort. Then, at the last minute, I gave Gordy Froehlich (a.k.a. Hummer) the fateful call.

Considerably older than me, a skinny dude best described as a duck-tailed, but balding Fonzi at 54, he was a professed pheasant hunter by avocation, and a good time-Charley by nature. Having gotten to know him at the gun club, I was always impressed by how he spoke so passionately of his many bird hunting trips in terms of the total experience, not just birds in the bag. It didn't take him long to sign on. And I was glad.

Seeing him walk up to my door the morning of our planned departure ... well ... I had second thoughts. In one arm he carried "all" of his clothes in two grocery bags, in the other his cased 1100 skeet gun. Behind him bounced his ill-mannered, (as we all knew it, but in his mind "highly trained") Springer, Shane.

All the while thinking, "What have I gotten myself into?" I quickly rifled through my gear, packing another goose gun for him, and enough extra, heavy clothes to keep his skinny butt warm on the prairie. It was my first lesson in having to look out for, and after Hummer, the lifelong adolescent he was.

So we set sail for NoDak with sky's-the-limit anticipation and good conversation fueling the way. Halfway across Minnesota I started to get a little groggy, so I asked Hummer to take the wheel. After a pit stop I closed my eyes and promptly fell off to never never land. It seemed only moments, but it was probably 60 miles later that I awoke to the lurch of a sudden lane shift. I was shocked to find Hummer, his head bobbing, groovin' to the tunes, with the driver's seat three-quarters reclined, and Shane on his lap. How he could see over the wheel I'll never know. I handled the driving chores from then on.

After a full day's push we arrived in the Kramer/Newburg area just before sunset. Taking advantage of the last available light we slowly cruised the backroads, where we took the wildlife extravaganza we encountered as a good omen. We spotted a bachelor group of whitetail bucks on the edge of a woodlot enjoying a wheatfield snack. As we slowly rolled along, we flushed four good-sized covies of Huns as they scratched for grit. And the whole time the skies were crisscrossed with flights of fowl. Wavering strings of snows and a few scattered flocks of dark geese winged low, to and from the nearby refuge. And several whirling clouds of ducks tornadoed stubblefields. All in all, it was quite a show.

After settling into the motel at Westhope we grabbed a coupla' beers and crashed, looking forward to whatever the morning would bring. What it brought first off, was a minor disagreement.

I awoke that first day, to the not-so-fresh aroma of dog dung, that I was dismayed to find the bathroom floor splattered with. Shamus kinda' cowered in the corner with his ears pinned back and a look on his face that said, "No. Not me boss." If he could've, I'm sure he woulda' pointed a paw at Shane, then sprawled smugly on Hummer's bed.

"Hey, your dog messed in the bathroom. Better get in there and clean it up," were my first words to Hummer that morning.

Grumbling all the while he did, muttering that Shane would NEVER do such a nasty deed, the black and white pooch calmly walked back into the jon and dumped another load right in front of Hummer's eyes.

"Well, I'll be. Can't understand what's gotten into him," Hummer groaned.

"Looks to me like all those greasy burgers you fed him yesterday," I laughed in reply.

Not having scouted for the morning's hunt, our only option was to hunker down on a rock pile in a field bordering the refuge, and hope for some pass shooting. The snows poured off the roost water in boisterously barking waves, but none low enough or close enough for us to take a poke at. So, after barely an hour, and seeing that he was shivering because he, "knowing better," hadn't dressed as warmly as I'd suggested, we opted to take a drive to see where the birds were going.

Pods of snows dotted the fields for miles around, but none appeared approachable. Until, off to the east, we found several hundred birds feeding contentedly, not too distant from a sparse, isolated woodlot. Stealth is another of those words I soon realized Hummer had no concept of. Trying to sneak those geese with the Old Dog and his old dog was all but futile. When the birds made us I took off on a mad dash for the open field. With three long, barrel-straining shots I managed a miracle, scratching down a pair of snows. Cripples both, Shamus had a great time running them down. Though he could have fetched one, Shane, much to Hummer's consternation, and considerable embarrassment, had no clue.

We scouted that same, somewhat remote field in the afternoon, happy to find even more birds using it than had in the morning. "This is where we'll set up tomorrow," I not so brilliantly told Hummer.

O'dark thirty found us ... well, me anyway ... hustling about the wheat stubble in the glare of the headlights, deploying our meager, 100-shell spread. Helping finally, with the installation of the heads, Hummer did one for my three at best. Better than nothing at all I guess. Not enjoying the task of setting a decoy rig was another of his weak points.

But the ol' boy sure could get excited. When a pair of early arriving juvies dropped from the still dark sky and flapped low through the high beams ... something I'd never seen before either ... he started mumbling something to the effect of "Awesome. Just awesome. Did you see that man? Awesome!"

After parking the truck a half mile off, I got back to the setup just as our first customers arrived. Hurriedly stuffing him into the field-edging dead-furrow, then joining him, I noticed Hummer shaking more than the usual product of his onsetting Parkinson's.

When that first boisterous flock of snows, 15 or 20 birds strong, all locked on tightly bowed wings slid toward us, I could hardly contain him. As I commanded, "Take 'em!," Hummer was right there with me, clamoring to his wobbly knees and cutting loose. Four dirty white-colored juvies smacked the stubble. Before the yellow dog could finish his job we had another flock in our face and four more birds down. Then again, with Shamus still cruisin' through the decoys with a white bird in his maw a pair of kamikazes first kited overhead, against the backdrop of a higher, whirling, barking mass of snows that were just "thinking about it," then tumbled wing over wing, righting themselves not 10 yards off the deck, smack in the middle of our spread. Two shots and we were done, with Shamus delivering the last bird just as the sun burst over the flat, endless horizon.

To that point the memorable morning's shoot had been the most outstanding snow goose hunt of my life. Yet it was one we amazingly duplicated the next day. Though not without one little hitch.

Shane, much to Hummer's chagrin, had continued to ignore the geese, holding them apparently, in total disdain. But when Hummer's shot folded our last bird of the morning, the there-to-fore grumpy old springer bolted toward it as if he'd been shot from a cannon. So did, as was his custom, Shamus. Arriving simultaneously, each took a firm hold on the goose. After an abbreviated tug-of-war, both dogs started to stumble toward us, each still clinging tenaciously to "their" goose. Something had to give. And in the end it was the bird. Both Hummer and I ended up with half a goose!

We couldn't help but laugh. And Hummer was obviously relieved that Shane had finally ... if a little late in the game ... gotten with the program. I couldn't help but chide him though. "Now, was that a retrieve? Or just a half retrieve?" I badgered him. "We might have to wait for next year buddy, but ol' Shane'll show ya," he cackled proudly in reply.

Well, it looked like I had a new running mate. One who had become quite the white goose expert, to hear him tell it throughout the long hours of the drive home. While that may not quite have been the case, one thing was certain. Hummer knew how to have a good time, birds or no. A lesson he taught me, that I still value today.

CHAPTER THIRTEEN

RVing for Snows

If our first trip together was spontaneous, then round two with Hummer was anything but. One of his longtime passions was his motorhome, and he more or less insisted we travel in its style. That "style" I soon learned, meant someone else ... usually me ... at the wheel, and Hummer on the couch, scratching his dog's ears with one hand while the other clutched a cold beer, all the while blabbering his entertaining life's philosophy.

With my truck on a trailer behind it, we were quite the impressive-looking rig. Anyone who saw it probably got the idea we were fairly well-to-do. Which would have been way wrong. Well-into-the bank was more like it. Hell, even then, most of our trip's budget went into the gas tanks. But it didn't matter.

Our goal was always to "give 'er" for those seven to nine days of the year's big hunt.

Being overly gracious, the Schepp's, Lynn, Martha, and their boys, Kevin, Kristen, Kyle, and Karson, let us park the rig in their yard for the duration of our stay. The bus served not only as our base of operations, it fast became our evening clubhouse. The conversation, jokes, and laughter we shared in its cozy confines, especially when joined by Lynn and one or more of the K-boys, was priceless.

Now, if you were a youngster into waterfowling at all, you would want to grow up on the Schepp homestead. Bordering the Clark Salyer NWR near Newburg, their land abuts one of the river's primary, fowl-holding pools. At almost any time during the season it provides some shooting for ducks, geese, or both. And at times of peak waterfowl concentrations, I'd have put those fields up against any, anywhere in North Dakota. Still, while Hummer, I, and Dave Warnke, who'd joined us that year, proceeded to enjoy a week of outstanding gunning, we were surprised to learn that the boys had never really gotten into a big shoot. Karson in particular, the youngest, most enthusiastic, and most outgoing of the bunch, would sit in drop-jawed amazement as Hummer regaled him with the play-by-play of our daily hunts.

It was only natural that Lynn and the boys had an open invitation to join us anytime their seemingly always busy schedules would allow. Which, the way things were going during our stay that year, didn't seem was going to happen. But on the last day of that trip, a Sunday, all four boys planned to hunt with us, at least until it was time for them to go to church.

It dawned a snotty, dirty morning, with a classically gusting prairie westwind topping 30 miles per, driving a ground-scraping scud that spit sleet in sporadic squalls. With our backs to the wind and our faces to the refuge, we'd find ourselves alternately wrapped in clouds of gritty prairie dust, or being pounded by micro-bursts of bead-shaped ice crystals. Either case making for a miserable, eye-watering, nose-clogging experience. With temperatures hovering right at the freezing mark we'd not have lasted long, had it not been for the geese.

I don't have any idea how many snows were roosted in the pool below us that day, but it was certainly thousands. Apparently reluctant to leave at first light, the barking of the birds would suddenly crescendo, and then, in a thunderous roar of wings, they'd blast off the ice-making water to aimlessly swarm up and down the river valley before settling back down, only to repeat the sequence again and again as the heart-stopping minutes wore on. Though raw and bone-chilling cold, it was the truly awesome spectacle we had front row seats to, that had us, man, boy, and dog alike, shivering in our boots as we laid huddled in the sparse, grassy cover of the fence-line, downwind of our decoy rig.

When that first flock finally broke our way we were more than ready. On they came, a family of snows seven birds strong, right on the deck, pumping for all they were worth into the wind and right at the boys. It took forever for the birds to get there, but when they finally passed low over them no one, NO ONE, moved. As the geese winged off I asked the obvious, "Why didn't you guys shoot?" To which they replied sheepishly,

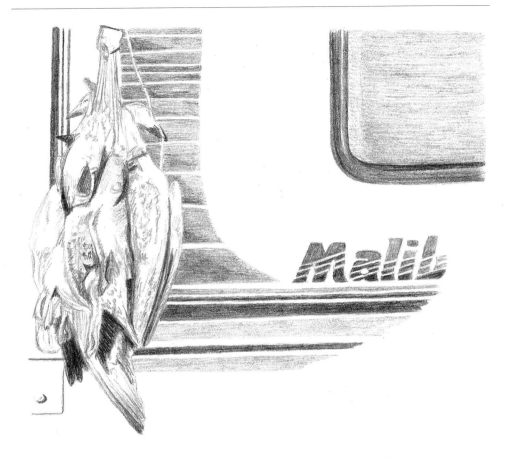

"Why didn't you?" It turned out we were waiting on each other.

"This in YOUR morning boys." I offered, clearing the air. "Take 'em when YOU got 'em. Don't worry about us."

Well, that did it. As the flight started to come in full force the boys were more than happy to cut loose, albeit with meager results. The combination of their relative inexperience and the puny steel loads in their 20 gauges had little effect on most of the geese. But the smiles on their faces as they tried, and the high fives when they did manage to pound a bird, were more than worth the price of admission.

After an hour or so of fast shooting Lynn walked out to join us. Or at least that's what we thought until he announced, "Time to get ready for church boys." Without so much as a grumble the well-trained, respectful lads started to gather up their things, not the least of which was a pile of yellow empties.

I'm sure it was the disappointed look on Karson's face that probably swung the tide. With cheeks glowing a wind-burned, fiery red, and framed by the ear flaps of his oversized cap, I watched as the young man's moist eyes met Lynn's, clearly begging the unspoken question. "Well, OK," Lynn relented, "I can see this looks like a special morning. I'll go talk with Mom."

Seeing their father striding back out only minutes later, and with gun in hand, the brothers let out a not-so-subtle cheer. So with Lynn joining us we proceeded to live large, experiencing a morning of mornings. Nary a minute went by without geese in the air nearby. And the boys kept blazing away, their stocks of ammo dwindling dramatically as the clock wound down toward the 1 p.m. closing hour. When the smoke finally cleared we had tallied 24 snows and blues as a group, the boys proudly accounting for all but a handful of them. With the weather becoming more brutal by the minute; we were content to retreat to the camper for the afternoon, torn between watching the Packers on TV, and the still-ongoing snow goose parade we could view out of the windshield.

With that year's hunt and its once-in-a-lifetime ending, the die was cast. Our annual return to the Newburg area would be one of the highlights of our hunting season for years to come.

In time we once again added some new and younger talent. An acquaintance of both of ours, Hummer and I welcomed Brian French to our crew. Ten years my junior, Brian, a waterfowl enthusiast and shooter of the first order, brought a refreshing, can't-sleep-at-night-for-all-the-excitement, perspective to the hunt. His was an injection of adrenaline that both Hummer and I needed.

In the history of our goose hunting adventures in North Dakota, Brian's timing, in terms of consistent, quality hunting, was pretty darn good. But my youngest son Jack's might have been perfect. Barely 14 at the time, when I offered, he gladly welcomed the chance to punch a week's worth of school to tag along. It wasn't that he was a gung ho hunter by any means. In fact he could quite well take it or leave it. It was likely the overall adventure, the promise of

a good time, and the opportunity to do something his older, chronically afflicted, nimrod brother hadn't yet done, that no doubt pushed his button. Whatever the reason, it didn't matter. I welcomed his interest and the opportunity to spend the time with him. Little did we know as we set out, what a great week was in store.

By sheer luck we had timed our arrival in NoDak to coincide with that of the year's first major push of snows. Topping it off was the weather. Not cold, but appropriately cool, each day proved a carbon-copy of that before, with a decent breeze and high gray skies. There was a ton of juvies that year, and every morning found them working our rig as gullible loners, in pairs, and in flocks of three, without adult supervision. Not shy about anything, Jack was pulling the trigger as much as any of us. Though his results, shooting a 3-inch 20 gauge at the generally tall birds, weren't up to par.

A wiry, slightly built kid, neither he nor I felt he was up to handling, much less banging away with a heavier 12 gauge. After going "O"fer early on, one otherwise highly productive morning, Jack put down his 20 and when not-so-seriously offered, surprisingly grabbed Brian's big 10 auto as yet another fringe-range single kited over the spread. Popping to his feet the little guy struggled to mount and swing the bulky, 10-pound plus canon. But when he touched it off that snow folded like a rag. Jack's bug-eyed look flashed into a broad grin. He shot a 12, and pretty darn well at that, the rest of the week.

In addition to the pleasure of having the youngster with, that trip is particularly memorable for its dog work. The pride and joy of my hunting life at the time, my Lab, Shamus, was pushing 11 years of age. The look in the gray-faced old warrior's eyes would tell me he was still up to it. But his sometimes-shaky legs would seem to say, "Maybe not." Though a downer, and sad to see, the boundless energy and wide-eyed, untempered enthusiasm of his daughter, Sadie, not yet a year old and on her first big hunt, more than buoyed my spirit. Alternating retrieves with him, and watching the veteran go about his work, Sadie learned quickly. Shamus would moan and groan when I held him back. But he was pretty stoic overall. Somehow, I felt he understood.

By that time Hummer, especially on slower days, wasn't always up for an all-morning hunt. Not an early riser by nature, he'd often sack in until he heard us gunnin'. Then, likely as not, he'd come stumblin' across the field, the skunk patrol, (by then he had THREE kids ... er ... black and white springers, ill-behaved, but spoiled and loved each one), bouncing along with him. He'd hunt for awhile, often taking his share of birds during the height of the morning flight, (the old fart could shoot), then, invariably claiming he was cold, he'd retreat to the motorhome. Where we'd find him, a can of Miller in hand, when the hunt was through.

When Hummer made his predictable move one morning, little Jack decided to go with him. No sooner had they disappeared than I saw my truck take off through the fields. They were up to something, but for the life of me, I couldn't figure out what. An hour or so later, here came my well-mud-died vehicle, rumbling along the fencerow from the west. As it approached it looked at first as if no one was driving. But then I finally made out the head of a low rider, Hummer's classically slouching profile I thought, behind the wheel. I was eye-balling some distant geese when the truck crunched to a halt beside me. Through the cranked-down driver's side window, in a pubescent, voice-changing croak came, "Hey Dad, how's it goin'?" Sure enough, the little guy was wheelin'. I stepped up to get a better look. There, fully reclined in the passenger seat, sprawled a devilishly grinning Hummer. "Thought junior could use a little driving lesson," the old, but perpetual teenager offered matter-of-factly. I could only shake my head and laugh. One look at the kid's smilin' face told me his fun meter was pegged. And that, I knew, was a memory-making good thing.

We enjoyed our best shooting yet on that trip. And for that it was notable. But it was the "everything else" that goes along with it, that made it so special.

Hummer, Brian, and I plugged away for several more years. And though we continued to enjoy some great hunts, never again did we hit it so perfectly. Things were fast changing in the Newburg/Kramer area. While it continued to host more white geese than ever, so too did it more white goose hunters. The increase in freelance hunting pressure, as well as that brought on by the several guide/outfitter operations that had sprung up in the area, added up to a ton of posted land and a major shift in the behavior of the birds.

The geese had learned that there was safety in numbers ... BIG NUMBERS ... and they began to move and feed, almost exclusively, in massive, essentially unhuntable flocks. No longer comfortable in flocks of mere hundreds, they staged and moved en masse, in swarms of thousands, sometime tens of thousands of birds. Reacting ever further to the severe hunting pressure stateside, the white geese lingered just north of the border, in southern Canada, later and later and later each year. Hunting them in North Dakota, something the state had become so famous for, and something which for so many of us had become such a grand tradition, was, sadly, all but becoming a thing of the past.

And for Brian and Hummer, by the early '90s, that's just what happened. Given our ever-poorer results, in terms of birds in the bag, I couldn't blame them for hanging it up. But I was still too stubborn, given the many years invested, and the sheer volume of priceless memories banked, to do so myself. No way could I let go of something so near and dear to me.

By that time in my life I had become a lot more flexible in terms of my schedule. I could pretty much go when the goin' was good. If that meant the last week in October, the first in November, or whenever the snows finally spilled into NoDak, I could get there to experience them. Fortunately, I once more found a couple of partners with the same ability. The first of these was my oldest son, Billy. Then a student in the natural resources program at UW-Stevens Point he could easily justify a "field trip." Gus Tarnowski, an old buddy and former work associate who had retired could do the same, and he welcomed the first-time-ever opportunity.

CHAPTER FOURTEEN

Gunning A River of Geese

The call from Lynn came early in the last week of October. "The geese are finally starting to pile in here," he said, adding, "with a major storm predicted across the Canadian prairies this week, one that's just going to skirt us here, the hunting should be prime." That's all it took. We were off and runnin'.

I was the designated wheelman as we tooled westward into the 14-degree chill of that late October night. It was only minutes after a late night pitstop to top off the fuel tank, but Gus' head was already bobbing in the passenger seat, and Billy, scrunched onto the crew cab's rear seat, was sawin' logs. Alone with the road, country tunes on the radio, and my thoughts, we rolled on through the flat expanse of Dakota prairie.

As we did, my mind flooded with memories of the many like-minded friends who had accompanied me over the years on this annual search for my personal Holy Grail: the sights and sounds of the snow goose migration, and a good shoot or two on its birds.

Hunting "the wild one" being what it is ... anything but a for-sure proposition ... I'd seen hunting partners come and go. Their first taste of prairie-goose hunting was rarely enough. They'd tag along until one year we'd get lucky, circumstances would be right, and we'd enjoy world class shooting. When followed by a year of frustration and mediocre gunning though, they'd politely bow out of the program. But I always understood. With Billy and Gus, I had my fourth different group in more than 20 years of traveling to the prairies. Knowing they'd be good company no matter how the hunt turned out, I was glad to have them.

While gunning partners had come and gone, the one constant over the

years had been my canine companions. It might be my fondest recollections are of the dog work. My first Lab, Shamus, seemed to live for his annual forays to the Dakota prairies. The fields, marshes, and potholes became his personal playground. And his daughter, Sadie, who road snugly, tucked away in her kennel box in the back of the pickup, had proved a carbon copy. Already in her ninth campaign, she'd had the good fortune to course the same turf, swim the same sloughs, and tremble at the sights and sounds of those same awesome flights as did her father.

The 15 hour drive had made for a long day, and the question that dogged me those last few miles was, "Why do I do this? Is it for the companionship? The shooting? The dogs?"

It was a question left hanging as I pulled up to our motel in town. Of more importance at the time was getting settled for a fast four hours of sleep before we had to roll out the spread.

Did you ever wonder what really goes through a dog's mind? Fifteen hours of truckin', four hours of sleeping in strange surroundings, then we drop the tailgate in a stubblefield and she pops out of her box with a bright-eyed but knowing look that seems to say "All right! Here we are again!" I'll never cease to marvel at a gun dog's unabashed enthusiasm.

We finished our set of shell and windsock decoys just as the day's first blaze of light began to ooze ever the eastern horizon. It was that one special time on each trip when a hunter's sense of anticipation is at its peak. What will the morning bring? Are the birds as numerous as we've heard? Will they come our way? What's it going to take to get them to work the decoys? Only time would tell. All that really mattered at the moment was that we were there.

With temperatures in the single digits and a prairie breeze puffing strong enough to make the windsocks dance, it was a decidedly "fresh" morning. But it wasn't until the first geese began to stir that a real chill began to run up and down my spine. Starting as a mere trickle, the flight soon blossomed into a river of geese flowing over the countryside. But the river ran away from us, and the first few hours of shooting time left both us and our gun barrels ice cold. By late morning the geese began to filter back to the nearby roost, and a few singles, pairs, and small flocks finally started to give us a look.

Gus had never hunted snows before, so we had him laid out downwind of the spread's landing pocket in hopes he'd get the best shooting. And he certainly did, but with poor results early on. The combination of birds smaller than the Canadas he was used to, kiting in from heights far taller than he expected, gave him grief. By the time legal shooting ended, we had scored seven birds, and Gus had managed one or two himself. "Not a bad start," I offered, to which Gus replied simply but enthusiastically, "Great day, great day!"

Over lunch at the local café I assured him we could've done a lot better. Gus countered with, "Hell, just seeing and hearing those birds was worth the price of admission. You know I'm not much with words, but what we witnessed today was truly a spectacle. One I know I'll never forget!" It was plain to see I'd picked a truly appreciative hunting partner, one who deserved what we were going to experience the next day.

Our second morning was one of those you'd swear would never dawn. Enough light eventually filtered through the heavy overcast to illuminate a gray, wind-driven scud that would spit icy, intermittent snow sqwalls. It would have been a thoroughly depressing atmosphere had it not been for the geese. The day's gusting westwind pulled the morning's first flights toward our field. While we never fooled a big flock, singles and pairs worked our spread from the onset of shooting time. The action was nonstop, too good to accurately describe. We all got our share of shooting, and I'm sure Sadie thought she'd died and gone to goose-fetching heaven. When she wasn't retrieving, she sat beside me scanning the skies with the dumbest looking doggy grin imaginable. Gus, who'd never been out of his home state of Wisconsin for any type of hunt, probably summed it up best when he solemnly commented, "This has been the waterfowl hunt of my lifetime."

It was hard to argue the facts. Gus, Billy, and I had each taken 10-bird limits of snows and blues in just over three hours of hunting. I'd hate to think how quickly we'd have been done had we shot better!

Further adding to the special nature of this trip was the fact that we were joined for the last two days by two of Lynn Schepp's sons, Karson and Kyle, along with their black Lab, Katie. Now I've had the good fortune of seeing these boys and their pooch grow from pups, and it's truly special to spend time with them in the field each fall. Having lived their entire lives literally right next to a refuge that will annually stage up to 200,000 geese and 50,000 ducks, you can imagine what type of hunters these boys and their dog have become.

Watching Karson in particular, was kind of like looking in the mirror. Of all the boys, it was obvious Karson had spent the most time with Katie. And it was clear that he'd come to feel the same about the hunt, and his canine partner's place in it, as we do. Katie shadowed Karson's every move. When Karson layed down, she'd lay right beside him. When Karson watched the sky, Katie's head would turn as if on a turret. When Karson shot, Katie became a black bullet. She'd mark the fall and have the bird back to Karson so quickly, it was hard for any dog to compete. Katie and Karson were naturals. And it's a special magic they shared.

While the gunning couldn't have been better throughout, perhaps the highlight of the entire trip came that last morning. We were hunting a field a scant half-mile or so from a major roost pond. Though we were once again close to a full bag, late morning brought a lull in the action. Then suddenly, several miles off in the southeast, a cloud of geese probably rousted by jump-shooters, blackened the horizon. As we watched they started to string our way. When the vanguard of the flock reached the edge of the river valley leading to the roost, they abruptly dipped low over the water and began to follow the channel northward. Flock after undulating flock followed-the-leader as they passed in review no more than a tantalizing 200 yards from us. At one point the raucous, white, gently flowing river of geese stretched for more than two miles.

The surface of the roost pond to our north soon turned solid white. But still the geese came, eventually towering into a swirling, roaring, tornado-like vortex, before settling among their brethren. I have no idea how many geese there were in that half-hour long parade ... 10,000? 20,000? More? But it was a sight that made our hearts race.

It occurred to me then that what we had just seen, heard, and felt surely held the answer to the question, "Why do we do this?"

Gus and I, and sometimes Billy, kept coming back to northern NoDak throughout the '90s, in an effort to replicate the experiences of that first special trip together. Try as we might, it couldn't be done.

We were frozen out. We were snowed out. But in the end we were driven out. Not forcibly of course, but rather by the decrease in the quality of the hunt.

Now, the locals remained as pleasant and hospitable as ever. But our fellow "hunters" ... well ... they'd become nothing more than truck-borne creepers. The geese, once they did arrive, got no rest. If a flock found a feed field it wouldn't be for long. Within minutes a convoy of pickups was sure to appear, its occupants promptly planning a jump- and-shoot assault.

Within just a few short years snow goose hunting in NoDak, as we'd known it, had all but come to an end. Sadly, this whole new generation of road hunters knows no better. If it sounds like I hold them in low regard, let's just say I have about as much respect for them as they show to the geese.

CHAPTER FIFTEEN

Bread and Butter Wildfowling

*N*ow, *there's no doubt that our adventures on the prairie were the highlight of each waterfowling year. But the bread and butter of our seasons, quite naturally, was the hunting we enjoyed as weekend warriors back home.*

As for our local hunting, it was a case of good news and bad. The bad news was that as the human population grew in our area, there was a proportionate increase in the amount of pressure brought to bear on our few, precious, public waterfowl areas. So much so, that for many of us, quality hunting on them ... save for that rare, midweek, late season day when the migration was in and the hunters weren't ... had become a thing of the past.

Still, the open water hunting on Lake Michigan remained as productive as ever. A fact not lost on the "kids." Steven Hiebing, John Butzen, and Clete Leonhard were big time into the open water phase of their waterfowling careers. In their typical fashion they were going all out, being the best they could be. Something they could finally afford, given that they had all become gainfully employed adults.

Well read when it came to wildfowling lore, Steve, the leader of the pack, realized that a layout boat ... a true, pumpkinseed-style layout, the type prominently used elsewhere in the country, but which was to his knowledge, nonexistent in his part of Wisconsin ... was what they needed. So he proceeded to secure plans for one; and, in the course of a winter's project, along with his two amigos, applied his carpenter's skills to producing an ultra-low profiled beauty.

Displaced by my work career to western Wisconsin at the time, I couldn't resist the kids' invitation to travel back east and sample some real layout gunning.

CHAPTER SIXTEEN:

Intro to Layout Shooting

It was early on a late October Friday afternoon that I met the boys at the Sheboygan harbor boat ramp. As far as duck days go, it was a beauty. Though sun-splashed, a howling 'noreaster had the protected harbor's outer water frothing, and abuzz with restlessly trading flocks of 'bills. And with no other hunters about, we had them to ourselves. It was a beautiful thing!

In short order the guys had the 16-foot utility launched and its motor hummin'. In its bow, covering a mound of decoys, rode the strikingly tiny, one man layout. John and Clete hopped aboard and idled out to anchor the layout, then strategically set the rig around it. With the hard work done, they returned for Steve and I.

Motoring up to the wave-washed layout, and with squadrons of scaup, apparently oblivious to our presence, already working the spread, Steve looked at me and announced, "You're lead-off old man!" At that I carefully clamored aboard the low-riding craft, immediately struck by its amazing stability. I knelt down as Steve passed me my shells and the skeet gun he'd insisted I'd bring. Knowing I had my doubts Steve implored, "Trust me. The open choke and the 7½s are just the ticket. We'll back outa' here and you'll soon see what I mean."

So I settled down into the little boat's below-waterline tub, with my head and shoulders propped up only high enough to put my eyes at sea ... er ... lake level. What a strange sensation! Never before, with the wind roaring over the top of me, and the harbor's short waves lapping at the bobbing craft's deck, had I felt so at one with the ducks' world.

But I had precious little time to give it more thought, as even before the boys in the tender had motored off, the birds were on me. There were 'bills from the right, 'bills from the left, 'bills whirling behind me, and 'bills boring straight in. It was surreal, a dream-like, almost out-of-body experience. But before I could get carried away, reality set in. Dreams-be-damned, I came up gunnin' from what effectively amounted to my hole in the water. With so many targets I decided to concentrate on the sunlit, black-headed drakes, not firing until I could see the gold of their beady little eyes.

Steve, as I should have known, was right on about the gun and ammo combo. The shooting was indeed skeet range close and fast, requiring the open choke with finer-than-usual shot. Even from the sitting position, it was high percentage and non-crippling deadly. But it could be painful, I quickly learned. Coming to the abrupt end of my swing on one right-to-left crosser, I nearly unscrewed myself at the hips. "If that's the sole drawback to layout gunning," I groaned to myself, "I can live with it."

My time at bat came to an end as my seventh bluebill of the then liberal limit splashed within reach of the layout. After netting the rest of the birds as they drifted downwind among a line of empty shot shell hulls, the boys pulled up and I was replaced. An experience of a lifetime, one burned deeply into my birdy brain, my hunt had lasted barely 15 minutes!

It's safe to say, though the opportunities were infrequent, I took my turn in the boy's layout every chance I got.

CHAPTER SEVENTEEN

Canada's on the Rise

*E*ven though I had the boat and a decoy rig for it, I no longer pursued Lake Michigan duck hunting on my own. I'd become a dog guy through and through. When it came to birds, if I couldn't hunt them with my four-legged buddy, I wouldn't. The rolling open waters of the big lake not only didn't require a dog, they were and remain, simply no place for one.

So what was the retriever-owning waterfowler supposed to do? A no-brainer, really, the answer was and remains hunt the geese!

While Canada goose hunting opportunity had been extremely limited during the period of my youth, (only 15 years earlier), by the '80s it was anything but. Thanks to blossoming populations of local geese, and ever-healthier flocks of migrants, we were allowed, outside of Horicon and a handful of intensively managed satellite areas, to take a goose per day, and during portions of some lengthy seasons, two per day per man.

Now, Canada goose hunting as we practiced it, (and believe me, we needed the practice), had its detractors to be sure. For those, going through the effort and expense of scouting birds, securing permission to hunt private ground, investing in a decoy rig, and learning how to use it ... all for "only one" goose ... just wasn't worth it. And I for one, was glad they felt that way. As far as our sport goes, they just didn't get it. For me, and other hunters of my ilk, the burgeoning opportunity was nothing if not heaven sent.

I can't even begin to recall how many great days we've had with eastern Wisconsin's Canadas since the '80s. I know it's only fallen

short of a lifetime's-worth because we're still here, above ground, and looking forward to the next one. But there are a couple that really stand out.

Opening day of the '89 goose season in eastern Wisconsin dawned warm, clear, and calm, anything but classic waterfowling conditions. The only possible explanation for the chill running up and down my spine could have been the constant gabbling of the several hundred honkers roosting contentedly on the Manitowoc River not 200 yards from where we hid.

Now, the credit for the fact that we were set up in such an ideal location goes solely to then hunting partner John Posey. John had done our homework by scouting the area and securing permission to hunt the 20 acres of sprouting winter wheat in which we had stealthily set our two dozen decoys under cover of predawn darkness.

With expectations naturally high, John, my youngest son, Jack, on his first goose hunt ever, and my then stiff-legged old Lab, Shamus, waited comfortably, but none-too-patiently in the tall, thickly woven willow patch bordering our field. The concealment it offered from both river-roosting birds and any passing birds we hoped to decoy, was near perfect.

As if on cue the morning flight began in earnest just as a stunning sunrise brought full light to the day. Singles, pairs, and small flocks were soon moving nearly everywhere over the surrounding countryside. Much to our surprise however, the geese roosted on the river stayed put. Far more attractive than our comparatively meager decoy set, the real McCoys soon become a magnet, pulling in a lot of the flight birds.

The geese working up and down the river really put our nerves to the test. They'd swing plenty low, and at times only 30 yards behind us, but always over the willows and the cattail marsh they bordered. Though it was surely tough, we opted to pass on those birds, stubbornly sticking to our pre-agreed plan. Our intention was to take only singles, or if we shot together, possibly a pair. But even then only if over the decoys. We felt it would make no sense to educate the larger flock, much less take the chance of accidentally hitting more than one bird.

John drew first blood when a single pulled out of a wide-swinging three-some and confidently cupped toward his side of the spread. The old gander pulled up short though, apparently sensing trouble at the last instant, and began to motor for the river behind us. John's 3-inch load of BBs intercepted the bird, sending it broken-winged into the heart of the willow thicket. Shamus, bolting at the shot like an adrenaline-crazed pup, tore into the tangle and soon cornered the still very much alive goose. Though we couldn't see the matchup, the brush began to shake with all the fury of a World Wrestling Federation cage match. The big, still heavily muscled yellow hound, a veteran of 11 seasons in the goose fields of Wisconsin and the Dakotas, soon emerged victorious; trotting toward us with the wing-flapping honker clenched firmly in his graying jaws.

Young Jack was on deck, and only minutes later he got his chance at what appeared to be a disoriented youngster, as it circled the spread once, then whiffled right in, presenting an in-your-face, head-on shot. I watched over his shoulder as the little guy mounted the over/under 20 gauge, then with his head far off the stock, whiffed with both barrels! Neither of us could believe it. Jack had been well practiced and nothing, as was his nature, if not confident.

Like letting the air out of a balloon, the kid's ego had been totally deflated. There was that needed period of silence before I calmly and tactfully tried to break the ice. After replaying the scenario in our minds, I explained, and he, though still moist-eyed and ego-crushed, understood what had happened. It was strictly a matter of not getting the "wood" on the wood. Though uncharacteristically straight-faced and sober, I could see Jack was determined to redeem himself if another opportunity presented itself. Which it thankfully did an agonizingly long half hour later.

A trio of geese, not about to commit, but giving us a close fly by, began to cross the spread from right to left. Without instructing him, I observed as Jack properly selected the closest and lead bird, matched its speed with his gun barrels, and then pulled a lead. When the 20 barked the head shot goose balled up as if it had run into a wall. I'm sure it was with a proud smile on my face that I managed to gather myself in time to scratch down the tail-end-Charlie.

The old dog seemed to revel in the easy retrieves. And all was well in our world.

After we packed up that morning we rendezvoused with a group of like-minded friends headed up by goose hunting fanatic, Pat Pentek, for breakfast. During the course of our conversation one of his successful group was heard to comment, "Geez, that was easy today." Pat's appropriate comeback was quick. "Yeah ... but remember ... its only easy when it works!"

It was those prophetic words that ran through my mind late in the morning on a hunt with him four weeks later. There were five of us that day, hunting our combined spread of 60 magnum-sized shell decoys. It should have been the hot setup. There was plenty of waste corn in our stubblefield. And the standing corn that rimmed its downwind edge provided an excellent hide for hunters and dogs. There was no shortage of geese either. But the localized, well-conditioned honkers had seen their share of hunting pressure throughout the season; losing a fair number of their buddies no doubt, to rigs like ours.

We were pretty much resigned to dealing with the agony of defeat when we began to notice a number of strato-high flocks, apparently late migrants, sliding down from the north. Only tentatively fingering his call at first, Pat muttered, "What the hell ... " then went to work, throwing every enticing note he could muster at the super tall birds.

I admit to being only a casual observer of the program of first. But after first one, then a second flock "broke" ... their V'd formations shattered ... things got serious. With his face reddened by the considerable effort, Pat, ever the field general barked, "Everyone down!," between calling sequences.

What a show it was as the towering, short-stopped, apparently weary and hungry migrants began to eyeball our rig. I don't know how high the geese were when we first spotted them, but it could only have been measured in the thousands of feet. What seemed like eternity probably amounted to no more than 20 agonizing, nearly breathless minutes as the 50 or 60 honkers total, at first tentatively circled the section, then, focusing on our field, finally swung cup-winged and totally committed into our trap. Not shooting well at all, we only dumped five birds in that first volley. But that was fine. Just to prove it was no fluke … though I'm not sure he knew what he'd actually accomplished … Pat repeated his virtuoso performance one more time. And that was enough for us to fill our late season two geese/man/day bag.

All in all, it was a hunt unlike any we'd ever experienced. Fairly exhausted, Pat probably summed it up best. "I'll take back what I said on opening day. It may have worked today. As for being easy? Well, it was anything but!"

PART FIVE

Reaching Out

*T*hough happy with it, and truly thankful for all it had given me, my wildfowling career ... if you can call it that ... had created a mid-life crisis of sorts. As far as the sport I so dearly love goes, I'd begun to dream of the impossible-to-achieve goal that would be experiencing every major waterfowling venue on this planet, at least once in my lifetime. To that end, thanks to having gotten to the point when I finally had the time and means, I began to reach out farther than ever before.

Surely the farthest stretch for me to that time involved an Argentine adventure in 1996.

CHAPTER EIGHTEEN

A Party in Patagonia

*B*rian French had been on my case for a couple years. "You gotta' come try the goose hunting in Argentina. There's nothing like it!" he urged. Proving his point were the thrilling videos he shot on each of his forays to the central Argentine province of Chabut. The action they recorded was enough to make this goose hunter's blood boil. But even more was the very idea of experiencing shooting unlimited, with no harm done to the resource, the geese being widely regarded as agricultural pests. That the gunning could be on a par with that of North America's halcyon days at the turn of the 20th century was intriguing to the max.

But Frenchie's hunts had taken place in June. And therein lay the rub. June is a precious month for me. All thoughts of wildfowl aside, my Junes are a time for fishing in general, and walleye fishing in particular.

"How about if we go in March?" Brian finally asked, then explained. "It'll be a much longer trip ... 7,000 miles one way ... to southern Argentina, Patagonia to be exact. There we'll hunt the geese on the breeding grounds before they migrate north to winter."

"Now you're talkin'!" I quickly agreed. March is probably the deadest time of year for a Wisconsin-based sportsman, so the timing was perfect. But even more, the prospect of a truly far-flung adventure was at the time, irresistible.

Brian handled all the planning, all the details. Pretty much all I had to do was show up. Something I hadn't anticipated would be so difficult. There was a nasty virus going around the office at work. It only figured

that it struck me with full-blown, pneumonia-like symptoms just two days before my scheduled departure. Buried with last minute projects, and no time to get to the doctor, I begged his prescribed drugs off my similarly stricken business partner, and was off.

Feeling every bit like I'd just been run over by a truck, we caught a plane in Milwaukee that Monday morning on the first leg of our journey. Little did I know the worst was yet to come.

I was hackin' and wheezin', with my eyes watering and sinuses throbbing as we boarded the Aerolinas Argentina 747 that evening in Miami, for the 8-hour overnight flight to Buenos Aires. Crammed shoulder-to-shoulder full with boisterous, cigarette smoking Argentineans still riding their Disney World high, it was the flight from hell.

Due to the sheer volume of our gear, disembarking in Buenos Aires was a hassle. Dealing with customs was easy enough. But getting our guns permitted was another story. Tucked away in a dark corner office in the basement of the airport, we struggled to deal with the paperwork, language being the assumed barrier. Brian knew the drill and had never had a problem before. Fortunately he was a far more worldly traveler than me. When he flashed a couple of 50-dollar bills, all was suddenly understood and settled.

After another 4½ hour jet ride south to the seaport town of Rio Gallegos situated on the straits of Magellan, completing a full 26 hours straight of travel, my butt was dragging. Our guide, Alec Byrne, and his sidekick, Fabrizio, met us at the gate. In no time we were headed through the nearby countryside to our first base of operations, the Estancia Truchaike. It occurred to me then that we were indeed a long way ... a very long way ... from home. "What have I gotten myself into?" was the question, trusting Brian's judgement, I kept to myself.

After dinner with Alec, during which he laid out our itinerary for the next few days, we were asked to sign the estancia's guest register. A quick glance through its yellowed pages showed it to read like a who's who of the fly fishing world. Names like Wulf, Brooks, and others were prominent. The area's rivers, I learned upon asking, provide storied angling for giant, sea-run brown trout. Fishing that draws anglers from all around the globe.

"Could the gunning in this remote part of the world be just as special?" I wondered. It was a question that would be answered soon.

The next morning we got our first good look at Patagonia, a place literature has defined as "the uttermost part of the world." Lying at the southern tip of South America, Patagonia, widely reputed to harbor some of the world's worst weather, had become a metaphor for the extreme, the point beyond which one cannot go. It seemed only appropriate that our quest for the ultimate goose hunt would take us that far, to this barren but strangely beautiful place.

As we motored in our two truck caravan, a shiny new rental Alec had ordered for the duration of our stay, and his prized '70s vintage, starterless personal rig, predawn's first light illuminated the stark, treeless countryside known as the "meseta" or steppes of southern Patagonia. It struck me more as desert than waterfowl country.

Not until Alec wheeled the lead pickup off the badly potholed asphalt and began to follow a fairly discernible two-track leading to the precipitous edge of an expansive valley did we begin to get the picture. While we paused briefly to take in the view, our guide explained that what lay before us was a chunk of real estate roughly four miles wide and 40 long. The floor of the valley, etched by a series of creeks, provided a rich, green contrast to the tawny, brownish gray tones of the grass-covered, scrub-laced pampas. And the healthy green grasses were full of life. Free ranging horses, cattle, sheep, and most importantly for us, concentrations of Magellan geese could be seen scattered throughout.

"Enough of the sightseeing," Brian intoned, "Let's get down there."

With that we plunged over the lip and rumbled downward, stopping short to park the trucks on enough of the hill to allow the old truck the roll it needed to start by popping the clutch. Alec knew where he wanted to set up, and in barely 20 minutes we had Brian's three dozen hand-painted shells and two dozen Magellan-imitating windsocks set.

Geese could be seen hopping around in almost any direction, their flights rarely taking them more than several hundred yards. With their food source sprouting everywhere, they had little reason to wing long distances. Noting as much out loud, Alec responded to my observation, "That's why we have to push the birds. Hopefully we can move them toward you and the decoys." The idea of having to haze the birds didn't sit well at first, but then it was a matter of "When in France ... er ... Patagonia ... " afterall.

As Alec and Fabrizio took off on the first of their many arduous hikes, Brian and I settled into our small, makeshift blind. The down jackets and GORE-TEX parkas provided welcome protection from the damp, penetrating winds. With temperatures barely nudging 40 degrees, there was a lot more bite in the air than expected.

Storm clouds began to brew over the western corner of our valley. But any concern for the weather quickly faded as the soft-gabbling Magellans began to filter our way. Brian gave me honors on the first bird, a big white gander that flared in striking contrast to the graying sky, at the last second. The fact that the goose took three solid body hits with the copper-coated deuces before dropping a full 62 paces distant, set the tone for the morning's hunt. So much for my concerns about totally gullible geese and too easy, in-your-face gunning.

The morning passed in a blur of barrel-melting action. By the time Alec suggested we break for a lunch of Patagonian T-bones we had the ground fairly littered with birds. The afternoon hunt was a little slower on the by then already-educated geese, but still beyond belief.

"No matter what happens from here on out, this trip is already an unqualified success," I told Alec. While he seemed pleased, he was quick to emphasize, "Oh, it can be much better. In this big valley the geese have too many options."

The next day found us set up adjacent to a fast-flowing creek at the bottleneck of a much smaller valley. The skies were clear but there was a gale force wind ushering in a coldfront from the west. The geese that worked upwind provided classic decoy shooting. Those that rocketed downwind with their afterburners lit provided uniquely challenging, if low percentage gunning.

The hunt was far faster paced than that of the day before. So much so that late morning found us, much to Alec's dismay, taking a break from the shooting, to work instead with the cameras.

After a light but pleasant field lunch of ham and cheese sandwiches washed down with the ever-present wine, we packed up and headed for Tapi Aike, a sprawling estancia nestled against the Chilean Andes, a 90-minute drive further west. After stopping at a school where the students enthusiastically took our birds, we rolled along, the truck rocking in the breeze. I commented on the tiring, persistently gusting winds. With a wrinkled brow and a shrug of his shoulders, Alec simply replied with a devilish grin, "Iss Paa-Taa-Gohnya!" Then he explained that in southern Patagonia, as a result of its proximity to both the Atlantic and Pacific oceans and their swirling currents that collide at Cape Horn on the southern tip of Tierra Del Fuego, only a couple hundred miles to the south, the singular constant in this country is the wind.

Pulling into Tapi Aike's courtyard, we were met by our hostess, Victoria. Next to Alec, she was the only other English-speaking person we'd met since arriving in Patagonia. After a few cervezas and a good meal, it was off to bed for a badly needed night's sleep.

We had only a 35-minute drive to Alec's chosen hunting grounds the following morning. But having to ford a series of rivers in the two-wheel drive pickups made the side-slipping trip an adventure in itself.

Upon arriving at our destination the reason for our considerable effort became immediately apparent. Spread before us was a relatively small, egg-shaped lowland that was alive with fowl. Audible in the distance, with a myriad of small flights moving about, the Magellans appeared abundant. And the numerous ponds were pockmarked with ducks, flamingos, and black-necked swans. With all the wildlife, and set against the backdrop of the jagged, snow and mist-shrouded peaks of the Andes just eight miles distant, it was a breathtaking scene.

With the rare occurrence of no wind, the unusual serenity of the morning was delightful. Setting foot in that valley ... one that Alec informed us had NEVER been hunted before, (How cool is that?) ... was a moving experience.

"It's almost too perfect to disturb with shooting," Brian muttered softly. "Almost."

At that the hunt was on. And once again the shooting was fantastic. But the scenery continued to be constantly more so. Between flights, I, ever-the-flatlander, was mesmerized by the ever-changing panorama of the mountains. Upon meeting the drier, more stable air on our, the arid Argentine side, the rolling, angry, variously gray-shaded clouds being blown in from the Pacific on the Chilean side of the range would dissipate, as if their moisture had been sucked up by some giant, mystical vacuum cleaner. The only time I took my eyes off the awe-inspiring show was when we had birds over the decoys. And that was often.

Alec put the wood stove in a nearby gaucho's shack to good use for a hearty meal of thick-sliced sirloins at midday. Suffering the effect of the wonderful meal, we needed a short siesta before taking to the field for the afternoon shoot. One which proved just as good, though a shortened version of the morning's. The following day would prove the high point, if we could really single one out, of the entire trip.

At daylight, after another pleasantly short drive, Alec had us overlooking an exceptionally narrow, but lush riverway. With the mountains fully illuminated by the sun rising into the clearest of azure skies, the wind began to puff, soon topping 50 miles per. But riding the gusts came the geese. Singles, pairs, small groups, and large flocks catapulted downwind, most, amazingly, swinging to work our rig on a low, final approach. We enjoyed shooting at every conceivable angle and distance while taking the opportunities as they came. With non-stop action, our biggest problem was keeping our guns loaded!

After Brian and I had gone through four boxes of ammo each, we called it a shoot. We could have run for more shells, but what would have been the point? Enough was enough.

The sumptuous meal of lamb chops Alex prepared on the estancia's outdoor grill really hit the spot early that afternoon. And the show the estancia's gauchos were putting on in the nearby coral provided a cultural interlude.

Dressed in their gaudy shirts, baggy black pants, traditional headgear, and cummerbunds sporting their trademark stilettos, the Argentinian cowboys whooped, hollered, and happily snapped their bullwhips with precision and skill, as they worked to separate colts from mares. It was quite the colorful show until they gang-roped one unfortunate youngster and pulled it down. As I watched in disbelief the head wrangler dashed in and slit the colt's throat, then casually walked away, his sopping shirtsleeve turned blood red. The gauchos cheered in unison.

Though a fact of everyday life on the pampas I suppose, it was a suddenly chilling scene. One that for me, took the edge off the moment. Only as I walked away did it occur to me. Maybe they don't shoot horses in Argentina. But they do eat them, don't they?

It was 5 p.m. that afternoon when Brian shook me from a particularly sound siesta. "Let's get goin'. We're going to do some filming," my video-happy partner urged. While it didn't take much effort to get me headed toward the field, I was more than a little taken aback, given my camera-shy nature, that Brian's mission was strictly to film me shooting.

We hunted a pasture within walking distance of the ranch that was bisected by a waist-deep, but dry ditch that provided pit blind-like concealment. The wind was still howling but the morning's clear sky had been replaced by one sporting cloud formations as spectacular as the mountains they intermittently hid. The birds began to work almost immediately. Their approach was the most confident we'd seen all week, a credit no doubt to our perfect hide and their habitual use of the hay field in which it was located. Though there was ample opportunity for downwind and tempting crosswind shots, Brian, to maximize his filming opportunities, insisted I take only incomers, and then only at close, frame-filling ranges.

While we accomplished what we set out to do ... film some action sequences ... my gunning left more than a little to be desired. My excuse was that of shooting a too tightly choked gun, throwing too big a load, at targets that were way too close. In reality, my lackluster performance was likely a result of stage fright. Even when I made a couple good shots, I'd go from hero to zero in the next sequence. Still in all, it was good fun.

The last day of our hunt proved a true Patagonian classic. It had everything from the persistent wind, to periods of sun mixed with those of a sleet-spittling overcast. The shooting was steady and, given that we were running low on ammo for the trip, the shots we took were high percentage out of necessity. We stayed in the field until nearly 1:30 before breaking for the final of Alec's feasts.

Though we had every intention of finishing the trip with an afternoon hunt, we could see that our guides, who by then had become our good friends, were, not unlike us, really beat. They had truly given us an all-out effort. Soon, conversation began to flow with the wine. It was then I suggested, and everyone heartily agreed, we call it a hunt. It felt good to just kick back and savor the events of the past five days.

So the much-anticipated hunt, in the wink of an eye, had come to an end. But not without leaving a series of deeply imbedded impressions.

When it came to adventure, the trip had been all it could be. And that's a credit to Alec and Fabrizio, a pair that proved as hardy as the land, and as tough as the wind itself. As for the shooting, little more can be said. Time will never erase the lasting impression that is looking over a gun barrel at a gale-driven flight of Magellans.

And that's pretty much what I briefly told Mary on a radiophone call later that afternoon. Hearing her far-too-distant voice over the scratchy, crackling, ancient phone set was a dose of reality. One that made me homesick.

With that memorable scene, I was more than ready to put the hunt in the books. Glad to have made it, even then I doubted I'd ever come back. But after making our first hop across the straits of Magellan to fill up the plane on Tierra Dell Fuego, I looked out the windows to see flocks of Ashy Head geese, the smaller cousin of the Magellan and a bird we didn't encounter, scattered along the edge of the runway. "Hmm ... well ... maybe if Ashy Heads were in the picture? Never say never Jack," I thought to myself.

CHAPTER NINETEEN

Hudson Bay... When Less is More

*A*s a little kid I pretty much devoured the monthly issues of the *Big Three:* Outdoor Life, Field & Stream, *and* Sports Afield. *Their adventure stories took me far, far away from North 12th Street in Sheboygan, to places I didn't even dare dream of ever visiting. Of all the wonderful tales related in their pages, none captivated my budding wildfowler's imagination like those that told of the marvelous goose hunting available on the shores of the great Hudson Bay. Pictures of turned up clumps of mud with goose wings added as decoys, sparse willow branch blinds, and deck-scraping flights of geese over the treeless tundra, are as vivid in my mind today as they were when first published those 40 some years ago. But it was the stirring accounts of the native guides and how they voice called the geese that intrigued me most.*

If there was one exotic locale I HAD to visit in this lifetime, it was the Hudson Bay Lowlands. On a fishing trip in Ontario I came across a flight service that offered a floatplane-based trip to the Shagamu River Goose Camp in the Ontario Provincial Polar Bear Park on the shores of Hudson Bay. Their brochure describing the hunt finally pushed my button.

The start to our adventure in Vermillion Bay didn't come off exactly as planned. With six hunters, all our ammo, gear, provisions, the pilot, and much to his chagrin, my Lab, Sadie, the severely overloaded single-engined Otter struggled to get airborne that calm, hot, and humid last day in August. After two nerve-jangling, failed takeoff runs, and with finally, only the slightest hint of a much-needed breeze, the big bird barely managed to

transition from water to wings, on a third.

After a five-hour flight over the scenic northern Ontario bush that included a solitary fuel stop, the community of Fort Severn, on the shores of the great Hudson Bay came into view. There Big Dave Smith, our pilot, cook, chief bottle washer, and social director swung the bright yellow plane to a southeasterly heading, flying low over the coast. It was as if we'd flipped a switch. In place of the seemingly endless boreal forest, below us spread miles upon miles of tidal flats bordered by the endless expanse of the rolling, frothing bay on the east, and by the classic, low spruce-studded muskeg of the Hudson Bay lowlands on the west. Over the tundra, in response to the drone of the Dehavilland's massive radial motor, rose a myriad of wildfowl. Flocks of snows and blues criss-crossed the landscape along with bands of Canadas. And wherever there were creeks, ponds, or marshes, ducks swarmed in unexpected abundance. But as we continued toward the Shag River, the quantity of birds disappointingly diminished to the point of scarcity.

Dave's perfect, much-more-difficult-than-it-looked landing on a shallow, postage stamp-sized inland lake a mile or so from camp was followed by a greeting from our guides, 74-year-old Jean Michel Hunter and 64-year-old Louis Bird. "Bird and Hunter ... hmm ... how appropriate," I quietly mentioned to hunting partner Steve Loebaka. The answer to our first and most obvious question, "How's the bird situation?" was both disheartening, and in typical native fashion, to the point. "Not many geese. There were, many, MANY last week. Between flights now. Maybe they come tomorrow," came the straight-faced Jean Michel's curt reply. Taken aback by his demeanor at first, we'd learn that the ever-serious Jean Michel was a man of few words. Now Louis ... well ... he proved another story altogether.

It was hard to believe. How could we have come that far north ... to the breeding grounds no less ... only to find the birds weren't there yet? "You shoulda' been here last week," was a bitter pill to swallow.

After getting situated in our clean but Spartan cabins and with the hunting season not opening until the next morning, Steve and I broke out the spinning gear and headed for the river. Our plan being to fish the Shag's sea run brookies while observing the evening flights of fowl. The fish cooperated. But the birds, save for the mergansers fishing with us, and a couple small flight of honkers, didn't. Without saying it, not wanting to throw a wet blanket on the party's fire, I was anything but optimistic about the morning's hunt.

Hunting three by three, our guides had chosen two locales near camp that traditionally produced snows, for our setups that balmy, summerlike opening morning. With the only geese seen moving, hugging the far off coast, the hunts were a bust. After going back to camp for breakfast, it was time to regroup.

It was obvious we'd have to relocate closer to the tidal marshes, and by early afternoon we'd made the four-mile trek in the camp's aging, far-from-totally reliable Argo. Hunting all together at first, a couple of us "experienced" snow goose hunters were anxious to deploy the several dozen windsocks we'd smugly packed along to bolster the meager spread of shell-type decoys our guides intended to employ. While Louis meticulously placed their well-worn, dirty shells right among the willows and blueberries at Jean Michel's native-tongued direction, we happily set our gaudy rig out in the mud-flatted open

I could see a scowling Jean Michel muttering away to Louis, who in turn only shook his head and shrugged his shoulder. When the first few passing flights, all small, family sized flocks of snows and blues, pretty much flipped us off ... even after our guides enthusiastic vocalizations ... did my light go on. Upon prodding him, Louis, the always polite, tactful spokesman, explained that the hunting we should expect usually involved working only one small group of birds at a time. "Most of the geese we hunt nest farther south along Hudson and James Bays. They're only beginning their migration as they pass through the Shag River area. But as they trickle northward to the major staging grounds near Churchill, from which they depart en masse for the prairies, they'll often stop here to rest and fuel up on our sedges and berries," Louis detailed.

"Hmm, so much for knowing it all!" I offered to Steve who was already on his feet, ready to pull our out-of-place set, then billowing gaudily in the breeze.

That done, we split up into two groups, each hunting over but a dozen strategically placed shells. Jean Michel's group, set up a half mile from us, got the first shooting. But it wasn't long before a wavering band of ground-hugging snows was headed our way. As Louis, with the customary twinkling look in his eyes, began to talk the talk, the geese responded, walking the walk. Between calling sequences Louis pointed to it then whispered, "The second, pure white goose, that's the leader. Shoot that one first." I stayed focused on that bird, wherever it floated among the 10-goose flock. When Louis, his chest heaving with the effort, made the call, I was lucky enough to do my job. As the rest of the flock flared wildly Louis went into the most excited, spine-tingling calling sequence I'd ever heard. Bringing the leaderless band of disoriented geese around time and again, even as Sadie scampered about making retrieves, we whittled away at them until there were only four geese left. "Enough," Louis finally announced. And we complied. "Not good to shoot them all," he explained.

There was no doubt this man of the muskeg had a link to his natural world that, only in time, this white man hoped to understand. Those few, mystical, almost religious minutes with that first flock of Hudson Bay snows remain unlike any I'd ever experienced before, or have since.

To prove it was no fluke, Louis and "his" geese entertained us with several repeat performances throughout the remainder of the afternoon. That amazing show alone, was well worth the price of admission.

Planning to stay the course, we set up along the coast again the second morning. There was a good number of geese moving up from the south early on. And we managed to take our share. But then the snow goose flight tapered off.

And that wasn't all bad. Steve and I had been distracted all morning by the clouds of ducks, and low-trading strings of Canadas we'd been watching a mile or so to the north. Louis seemed mildly amused, but crusty old Jean Michel was obviously PO'd by our interest in them. Snows and blues were his game. One he obviously took great pride in playing.

A couple guys from Jean Michel's group broke ranks first, though. When they started bangin' away in the distance, Steve, Sadie, and I were quick to follow. After a short hike we found ourselves in puddle duck heaven. At first we just watched in awe as massive flocks of pintails and greenwings flushed and wheeled over the ankle-deep tidal pond, only to suddenly settle on the exposed mud flats. Once down, their numbers drew flights of mallards and the occasional small knot of blacks. And it wasn't long before the ducks were joined by two or three hundred cacklers and several dozen of what appeared to be giant Canadas.

We simply hunkered down in a patch of shore-side willows in the hope of getting some pass shooting. The action wasn't long in coming as a flock of 30 or so 'tails buzzed our point on a downwind rush. We managed to scratch down a bird apiece, much to the relief of the always eager pooch who was acting anything but her age.

With our opening volley the expansive puddle erupted as the teal strafed, the pintails swarmed, and the silvery underwings of the mallards and blacks flashed overhead, illuminated by the bright afternoon sun. The dark geese initially headed for the rolling bay, but in minutes began to drift back, a few small flocks at a time.

Having put ourselves smack dab in the middle of a world of wildfowl, we were faced with the pleasant dilemma of figuring out how to get the most of it. To prolong our pleasure, we quickly decided to employ only one gun at a time. By propping up our first few birds on the mud, their heads wedged into short, pruned willow branches, as those articles studied in my youth had illustrated, we had all the decoys we needed for the naïve birds. Passing on the teal, Steve and I concentrated on big ducks to fill our limits. The geese cooperated as well, and before the afternoon was out we'd taken Canadas of four distinct races, including a pair of 12-pound giants.

That wonderful hunt passed all too quickly. But its priceless sights and sounds were forever burned into our brains.

Our last day dawned wet and dreary, with a low, rain shower-laced scud being driven over the lowlands on the teeth of a gusting, northwesterly blow. There were absolutely no snows moving, so once again the duck hunt was on. And it was a dandy! With the whole group hunting the same flat, Sadie was more than happy to work for all the guns. Fortunately for her, the going was easy. There were no super long or highly technical retrieves required. Still, for the white faced 10½-year-old veteran, who was smartly and efficiently fetching two ducks at a time, it proved a helluva start to a season that would prove her retirement party. Even Big Dave, who'd joined us for the morning shoot, commented that the yellow dog had worn a soft spot in his heart. One that generally had no room for canines.

By late morning the breeze relaxed, the sun parted the clouds, and the birds quit moving. While everyone else decided to make the Argo-trip back to camp for lunch, I opted to stay put and hang out with my rightfully tired old hound. After hiking to its very shore, just to be able to say we'd actually set foot and splashed about in Hudson's Bay, Sadie and I strolled back to our willow bush hide, curled up together, happy but fatigued hunters both, and promptly fell asleep.

I thought nothing of it, but when the boys came back out, led by a frowning, agitated Jean Michel, who came charging across the pond on suddenly youthful legs, his battered old, but useless 30/30 lever gun in hand, I knew something was up. And it wasn't good!

Rising to my feet as he drew near I could see the relief in Jean Michel's cataract-clouded eyes. Seeing me alive and well he spoke in English for only the second time all trip. "Never, never alone with dog!" He grumbled, no doubt rightly thinking, but keeping it to himself, "Dumb white man."

Louis, who'd taken quite the verbal beating from his elder later explained. "Polar bears have an especially acute sense of smell, and an appetite for dogs. That's why none of us in camp have any. They only serve as bear magnets."

The afternoon hunt was slow and that was fine. It gave us a chance to talk with Louis and learn more about him, his people, and the wonderful, distant land in which they lived.

A most willing communicator, Louie explained ... all the time scratchin' Sadie's ears, and her lovin' every minute of it ... that his chief vocation, aside from his people's standard professions of hunting, fishing, trapping, and guiding, was that of the tribe's storyteller. In that capacity he'd made it his life's work to record and eventually publish, in both English and his native language, the entire "legend" or history of his people, thereby preserving it forever. He regaled us with stories of his learning-to-live-off-the-land youth. And his eyes just flashed when he spoke of times long past, such as the day a much younger and stronger Jean Michel last harpooned a Beluga from a freighter canoe out on the open bay. But they teared up when the subject turned to his people's present day youth. "A lot of our younger people don't seem to care about the old ways," he noted sadly.

Adding, "We can't even get our youth interested in learning the language of the geese. That's why we, old men, are here with you."

While he had a lot more to say, he emphasized that his people are not Cree at all, but rather Omushkigowack (people of the muskeg). "Why then," I asked, "have I always read 'Cree?'" "Probably because you writer-types find that word easier to use!" he replied laughing, no doubt thinking he'd gotten one up on me. Which I suppose he had.

Time spent in conversation with Louis Bird was an unexpected bonus on this hunt, as were the polar bear sightings on the flight out the next morning.

Just after lift-off Dave pointed the Otter toward the coast, barely skimming the treeless tundra. We weren't airborne for a minute when he excitedly pointed out the windshield to the 12 o'clock position and announced, "There. Look. There's your bears. Three of them!" Sure enough, barely three miles from where Sadie and I had napped the day before, was a huge mama bear with a pair of year-old cubs. Dipping the right wing in a steeply banked turn, Dave circled the trio skillfully at a scant 100 feet of altitude. We all got a good look at one very angry bear. Standing menacingly on her hind legs as the mud-caked cubs jostled for position, trying to take cover under mom's substantial, creamy colored bulk, she clawed and pawed at the air as if challenging the noisy, annoying, big yellow bird to come any closer. It was quite the show. But we all agreed we'd come close enough, Sadie and I in particular.

And so our short, sweet adventure had come to an end. Our effort to save the tundra had come up a little short, only because we didn't have the opportunity on the geese ... due strictly to vagaries of nature ... that we expected. But the duck hunting was more than we could ever have hoped for. So it goes. And I guess it's a good thing it does.

CHAPTER TWENTY

North to Alaska...
A Wet and Wild
Fowling Adventure

*I*n *truth, I'd never given Alaska much thought. Alaskan adventures, by their remote nature, require a high cost of travel. With such priorities as raising a family, putting kids through college, and planning financial futures, it seemed Alaska would be something Mary and I would do in our golden years. Then too, bird hunting, primarily waterfowling, had always been my first love, more or less directing my shooting life. Because Alaskan hunting, in my mind anyway, had always been synonymous with big game, it took me awhile to realize our largest state had some very unique and high-quality bird hunting to offer. Still, my research into it was only casual at first.*

But when I finally connected with Rick Reynolds, a lifelong Alaskan who I could sense was as waterfowl-driven as I was, I thought I might be on to something. Speaking with his sidekick, a young Minnesotan by the name of Levi Hendrickson, I was sure of it. Hardly needing to twist their arms, Steve Loebaka and my son Billy signed on for the adventure.

We first met up with Rick at the King Salmon airport. Never knowing what to expect when you meet a guy face to face for the first time, Rick didn't disappoint. Greeting us as if we were long lost friends, Rick, at a sturdy six feet, bearded, and with a bushy head of yellow hair that we'd learn wouldn't be topped with a hat no matter how wet the weather, struck me as the epitome of the second generation bush pilot, commercial fisherman, guide, and jack-of-all-necessary Alaskan outdoor trades he'd represented himself to be.

Wasting little time, we carefully crammed our gear into Rick's prized, dark blue 185 and were off, flying southwest along the Bristol Bay coast. We had no sooner settled in to enjoy the ride when things got interesting. When Steve spotted a big brown bear strolling along the beach Rick reacted, putting the Cessna in a steep, descending turn that pinned us in our seats and put us barely 50 feet above the bad boy's head. Apparently not happy about the company the bear stood up, assuming a posture that seemed to say, "C'mon, just try me!" After a second photo pass we winged on.

With Pilot Point's distinctive shoreline looming in the distance Rick swung inland to survey some of the endless ponds, marshes, and lakes that pock mark that part of the Alaskan Peninsula we'd come to hunt. While his favorite areas showed good numbers of ducks and what we thought to be plenty of geese, Rick offered that he was disappointed. "The cacklers aren't here in the numbers they should be. It being only the tag end of September, and given our unusually mild weather, you're probably a little early. Ah ... but we'll still be OK," he reassured us.

I looked at Steve thinking, "Where have I heard this before?" Reading my mind he only nodded and grinned.

Just before landing, and right on the edge of town we flew over an open, willow-brushed hill that sported no less than nine brown bears, including two sets of mamas with twins. Rick noted that "bear hill," with all its berries, was a great spot to find some ptarmigan if we were interested. "Oh, don't worry about the bears. They'll scatter when they hear the bikes (four wheelers) coming," Rick said in all apparent seriousness. That he did spoke volumes about the hunt to come. As for those ptarmigan, they were safe.

Levi was there to meet us at the Old Pilot Point air strip, where Rick maintained a hangar. Bubbling over with enthusiasm, he looked, with his

fair, rosy-checked complexion and spare, fuzzy whiskers, even younger than his 18 years. The fact that he had to pop a Duck Commander (his professed hero) tape into the lodge's video player even as we got situated, spoke volumes about his pure love of our sport. As for his knowledge? Well, we'd soon find out.

After changing into hunting duds and grabbing a quick sandwich, the five of us, along with Rick's half Lab, half Wiemaranner, Judd, headed out. From the launch site it was a short jet boat ride across Dago Bay to the tidal flats the boys had chosen to hunt that first afternoon. Hitting the beach we could see a bunch of geese feeding on an eelgrass stand exposed by the low tide, barely a half-mile off. Rick wanted to simply jump the birds, hoping, with the group spread out in the downwind cover, to pass shoot them, when and if they returned. Rick's plan struck me as odd, but I thought little more of it at the time. Levi, I was pleased to see, was not shy about getting into the mix. He argued, and rightly so, the merits of quickly deploying a decoy spread to work the birds within range of all the guns. I sided with the young man. After deploying our small rig, a Duke's mixture of floaters, shells, and silhouettes, we hunkered down in a thick stand of taller, but still wet and salty grass to wait. It wasn't a half hour later that the first wave of 30 cacklers, totally sold by their Judas brethren, swung low over my hide on stiffly locked wings. Two of my three shots connected. Judd had no sooner collected the pair than the second bunch arrived. Once again my stars were aligned, and as the birds hung at less than 25 yards I took an easy right and left, filling my four-goose limit.

Just like the rest of the crew, Rick had yet to fire a shot. But unlike the other boys, he appeared visibly frustrated, a hint I'd learn, of his competitive nature.

Not unlike ducks flushed from a prairie pothole, the geese continued to stream back to us, and everyone enjoyed great shooting that glorious afternoon. One that with Belugas and seals rolling and playing in the sparkling waters of the bay, and with untold flights of fowl filling the azure sky against the dramatic backdrop of snowcapped, volcanic mountains, will be forever remembered.

After the goose flight ended Levi plopped a dozen mallard blocks on a nearby pothole, and in short order we had a decent little duck shoot going. But with the high tide finally threatening to overtake our position, and the bright sun setting into the sea, we had to call it. It had been a beautiful day in Alaska. The last weatherwise, we'd see for five days.

We hunted the Dago creek flats again the second day, our results roughly duplicating those of the first. But by the end of the rainy, muddy hunt, it was evident we'd pretty well educated the birds in that part of our fowl-filled world.

Over a timely pintail dinner that evening, and with a devilish gleam in his eye that should have warned us, Rick announced, "Tomorrow we're going to introduce you boys to the goose flats. Then," he challenged, "we'll see if you're really up to what our Alaskan waterfowling is all about."

To get to his beloved flats we needed to use Rick's 22-foot aluminum sea skiff. Though stationed high and dry on the beach since the summer's commercial fishing season, launching it would not have been much of a problem had it not been for the gusting 30-knot winds and the resulting surf pounding the beach. Getting the big tub in the water proved a daunting and drenching task. One Rick, who in his ever-Alaskan, we-do-whatever-it-takes, matter-of-fact manner, made little of. After launching and deftly handling the awkward craft in the breaking rollers, it was obvious Rick's seamanship was at least on a par with his ability to fly a bush plane.

Once out on the flats it was a matter of going with the flow. Rick dropped us off one at a time, one half to one mile apart. His instructions were simply to, "Walk at least an hour in from the beach. Then look for birds trading and try to position yourself to pass-shoot them."

Slogging in waders through ankle-grabbing sedges and grasses, some as high as my head, and having to struggle across tidal creeks, their bottoms paved in slimy, greasy, stinking, boot-sucking salt mud, often as deep as my thigh, was for me and my arthritic back, like being on a death march. But true to Rick's word, the further inland we pushed the more birds we encountered.

I could hear Rick, and sometimes the other guys, sporadically bangin' away in the distance, throughout the very long day. But I held off shooting until I finally hooked up with Rick and Judd later that afternoon. Though I'd had opportunities aplenty, I knew my nose didn't work well enough to find birds dropped into such thick cover.

With the day's persistent wind and intermittent rainsqualls it had been one tough, grueling hunt, as nasty as any I'd ever endured. In some perverse way though, just surviving everything wild Alaska had to throw at us, made it worthwhile. And to a man, we could see the potential. Drop some blocks on a prominently used pond, or set a rig of silhouettes out on a mud flat, and we might be in business. One thing was for certain. This Alaskan adventure would involve no gentlemanly jaunt to a heated pit or blind. We were in for a dose of hardcore, mud-from-head-to-toe, work-your-butt-off, wet and wooly WILD 'fowling.

We took the next day off ... we needed it ... to do some fishing for silvers. Nearly as exhausting as the hunting, we fished till we almost dropped, hooking, playing, and sometimes landing one super tough salmon after another. But even as we did, thoughts of those intimidating goose flats rolled through my mind.

While enjoying the best salmon dinner I'd ever tasted, a plan came together. Having come to understand by then that competition and one-upmanship was part of Rick's game, one born of having to be among the best just to make a living in the Alaskan outdoors, I challenged him, wagering some insignificant amount on who would do better on his flats the next day. Knowing full well how much I liked to hike, and beaming from ear to ear, he jumped all over the idea. Billy and Levi, the young guns of the group, were willing to go heads up with Rick. But Steve and I had something else in mind.

Motoring along the next misty, dreary, low-skied morning I turned to Rick and asked him to let Steve and I out first. As we scuttled from the boat we each grabbed a sack of goose silhouettes. Rick frowned, but Levi and Billy nodded knowingly.

We'd been there and done this before, Steve and I. By the time our three Amigos were on their walking, slogging way, the two of us had high-stepped no further than a block inland from the beach and deployed our rig. Even with a ground mat we were soon mud-caked as we layed out in the only available, short grass cover. But almost as quickly, we were covered up in fowl. We hunted quite casually, taking the birds, ducks and geese, as they came, only one of us shooting at a time. But we were done, having taken full limits, hours before our buddies returned. Billy and Levi, having worked together, had their birds too. And that was good. Rick, fittingly enough, had come up a little short. But all of them, including our erstwhile robust leader, looked pretty pooped. It was obvious the demanding day on the flats had kicked their butts. Steve and I, having wallowed around in the slime, were just as grungy ... maybe even more so ... but we were still fresh.

There wasn't a lot of discussion about our bet that evening. There didn't need to be.

Rick, always the good sport, rightly acknowledged his defeat, in his own begrudging way, by joining us for some classic decoy hunting the next and last day of our trip. We'd done it his way. It seemed only right he did it ours.

As if to put an exclamation point on the rough and tumble hunt, everyone shot exceptionally well. Doubles were common and clean kills the rule. It was his saving grace that Rick bagged the most birds with the fewest shots. Something we'd never have known had he not kept score.

And so our Alaskan sojourn had come to an end. Thanks once again to our wonderful sport and the wide world of wildfowl in which we pursue it, we'd made new friends and experienced an amazing adventure.

As much as anything though, this trip will be remembered as a week in waders. Southwestern Alaska we learned, is a soggy land. Whether hunting or fishing, to deal with it you'd better be well-booted. But to see, feel, touch, and maybe even become a little part of this wet and wild corner of the Greatland, was truly something special. Far more than worth the substantial effort.

CHAPTER TWENTY-ONE

A Rice Field Reunion

*L*ate season, Southern-style duck hunting ... the type Gulf marshes, sprawling rice fields, and flooded green timber is made of ... had been something I'd always looked forward to. Someday, when I had the time, I intended to sample it. A call from my long lost huntin' buddy, Dave Kovacic, suggested that time was at hand.

Since our early days life had taken Dave and I down different roads. But we had always managed to stay in touch, even getting together to fish, shoot, or just B.S. for a day or two here and there. With Dave, as in life, some things never change. One thing that's always remained a constant with him is his unpredictability. You never know what he'll come up with next, what he'll wholeheartedly get into, or why. That's why, when after a nearly 30-year absence from any serious waterfowling, he suggested we look into some Cajun-style ducking, I wasn't all that surprised.

A road construction foreman spring through fall, Dave spends his laid off winters in far northern Wisconsin doing a little snowshoeing, a lot of snowblowing, building boats in a bottle, and generally just thinking. Which is to say, not a lot. So while he had the time, I decided to make it.

"You bet buddy," I replied. "I'm on it!"

And that's how we found ourselves headed to southwestern Louisiana ... renowned Cameron Parish to be exact ... early that January. Our goal being to intercept a few of the 4.7 million 'fowl the latest estimate had put wintering there.

After a short drive through the flat, featureless, pitch-black countryside, we stepped from our truck into the starlit Louisiana night. Fresh down from The Great White North, we were struck by the temperature, which though only in the high ’40s, felt balmy.

As my son Billy, Dave, and I stretched our legs and made small talk, we felt no need for our hunting coats. That's why we got quite a chuckle out of seeing our young guide, Mark, come wheelin' around the corner of the barn on his ATV with his quad parka buckled up so tight that only his eyes and nose were showing. I'll swear his teeth were chattering as he sternly told us, obviously not seeing the humor in the situation, to follow him on down the lane.

So follow him we did, along a two-track that bordered a series of dry, harvested rice fields. We eventually passed a number that held both water and ducks, which promptly erupted under the gaze of our high beams. After arriving at our hunt field Mark directed me to park the pickup next to a distant pump house while he ferried Billy and Dave across the ankle-deep water to the waiting pit blind. Then it was my turn to hitch a ride as my young Lab, Tanner, splashed alongside wearing a particularly bewildered look. For a dog of only 15 months, he'd already been exposed to a wide host of situations during our hunts on the northern plains, but this was something entirely new again.

Settling into the cozy, welded-steel blind sunk into a levee, I slipped my gun from its stiff case, which I in turn slid out of the way along the back of the blind, barely creasing Mark's backside as I did. "Geeeezus!" he exclaimed, coming totally unglued, nearly jumping outa' the blind in a rare expression of emotion. One that thoroughly shattered the stillness of the quiet morning. "What the ... ?" Dave asked. "Man, I thought for a second we had a 'gator in here with us!" Mark sheepishly replied.

Talk about culture shock. We'd never even given the cold-blooded critters (snakes and alligators) a thought. But from then on, we certainly did.

Despite the bluebird weather pre-dawn showed we'd have, flocks of ducks could be seen trading in every direction and at every altitude, back-lit by the pinkening sky. And those birds we couldn't yet see generated an auditory overload. The jet-like roar of pinions shredding the thick, damp air, the raspy quacks of hen mallards, the soft whistles of pintails, the hair-raising "la-lack, la-lack" of specklebellies, and the distant clamor of a swarm of snows, punctuated our world of wildfowl.

Anticipation ran high as shooting time arrived, but it was soon apparent the calm weather was going to work against us. The ducks were interested in our field alright, but the motionless 80-block set proved none-too-reassuring, inspite of Mark's constant calling.

Without a breeze on which to work them we grudgingly realized we'd have to take our birds on the swing. Dave, (geez, it was good to see him at "work" again), and Billy picked their shots as I struggled to keep a tightly wound Tanner under control. First Dave smacked a nice bull sprig, then Billy popped a greencap as it chased a Susie across the far corner of our spread. And so it went, a teal here, a wigeon there, as we quite contentedly picked away at what the morning offered, with one notable exception.

Mark made it clear, in no uncertain terms, that the hell-bent-for-leather spoonies that constantly bombarded the set, were off limits. "There are ducks, and then there are shovelers," he explained authoritatively. There was no room for discussion.

Tanner thoroughly enjoyed the work but only got more fired up as the morning wore on, trying somewhat short-fused Mark's, and as a result, my patience. Now, I was there at least as much for the dog work as the shooting, willing to sacrifice some of the latter in exchange for the experience the young dog would get. Mark, steely eyed, straight-faced, and generally humorless, was strictly into his perceived job, that being killing ducks, first and foremost. A fidgety dog, still on the front half of the learning curve, was a detriment to his single-minded cause. And without coming right out and saying it, he let me know his feelings. Too bad he didn't understand his customer's priorities should have come first.

Tanner eventually settled down. Enough for me to get in a little shooting and bag a fine pair of greenheads myself.

By 9 a.m. we were down to swatting mosquitoes. Not a pleasant task, but one we could rightly brag about doing in January, to our snowbound buddies back home.

When dealing with Mark over the phone prior to our trip he made one thing clear. "If you like real Cajun cookin', then the one thing we CAN guarantee is that you'll get the best, and plenty of it!" The meal of crawfish etouffee' and deep-fried shrimp that his wife, Sippi, had waiting for us after our first day's hunt proved his point. Talk about having to roll rather than walk away from the table!

Mark ... maybe a little frustrated with us, maybe committed to his other customers ... handed us off to his partner, Jack, on day two. At only 25 years of age, Jack was seven years Mark's junior. Though easier going by nature, it was apparent the two had gone to the same school of the great outdoors.

The second morning dawned a warmer, but otherwise carbon copy of the first. The only difference being a major lack of birds. Shooting straight at every opportunity, we killed but a handful of mallards and greenwings. Needlessly apologizing for a Mother Nature over which he had no control ... and had yet to realize that he never would ... young Jack offered, "We can give'er a shot again this afternoon if you boys are up to it." Though tough duty, after having been stuffed with a hearty midday meal of red beans and rice topped with smoked sausage, we were.

When we pulled up to our appointed field things looked pretty promising. There were perhaps 150 mallards and half that number of smaller ducks on the water. Flushing the birds, we expected them to trickle back. But we soon learned this wasn't Manitoba, Saskatchewn, or North Dakota. The fast-departing birds apparently found other, readily available roost water to their liking, leaving us to monitor skies graced only with flap-n-glides ... Jack's term for the ever-abundant egrets, cormorants, and herons ... during the early going.

Though rarely successful, except during periods of rough weather he explained, Jack, never short on ambition, began "hollerin'," (the Cajun version of voice calling), at the sporadic flights of snows that began moving late in the afternoon. As if to justify our guide's substantial effort, a single juvie snow peeled out of a skyscraping flock and began to ever-so-cautiously circle our rice paddy. Though plenty tall, the goose made the mistake of swinging over our hide once too often, and I busted it much to Tanner's delight.

With that goose and the afternoon's lengthening shadows our luck with the ducks began to change as first a single greenhead, then a pair with a hen worked to Jack's persistent pleading. Time was running out when, with barely three minutes of shooting time remaining Jack got a flock of

14 or 15 mallards on the string.

One pass. A second. Then a tentative third. And finally, here they came, fully committed and all cupped up. For once we had 'em in our face and we made the most of it, dumping four fat green caps and one mistake Susie in a day-ending volley. There were high fives all around as Tanner splashed happily about his business.

Back at the ranch, after a prolonged cocktail hour and a hearty meal of Cajun shrimp fettuccine, sleep came easily.

With clear skies once again for our third and final morning of the hunt, we held our expectations in check. After a couple opening-minute flurries with full-colored greenwings that tried to fly our caps off, things slowed right down, save for the spoonies. With a simple, "what the hell!" Dave surprised us all, dropping a handsome pair of full-colored, shovel-beaked drakes. It was vintage old, sea-ducking Dave, and a beautiful thing at that. Oddly enough, Jack seemed to mind not at all. So we all cut loose on the next flock, concentrating on the brand "X" greenheads. Just like us, Tanner apparently cared less that his mallards were "smilin'." Billy had smacked a neat double this time, prompting Dave to tag him spoonBill, for the rest of the trip. And the youngster wore the label well.

We were all about simply having fun that morning when, about 9 a.m., something really unusual happened. A nice, fresh, mosquito-chasing breeze began to kick from the northeast.

Rather than just dead air and flights of flap-n-glides, the clouding skies soon sported ducks and geese in abundance. And Jack did his best to make sure we got our share. What a difference it made to finally have a wind on which to work the birds. Time flew as fast as the shooting that developed.

The highlight of the day came when Jack sweet-talked a flock of specks close enough for Dave and Billy to get a crack at 'em. They each took a solitary, bar-bellied beauty, their first ever.

After one last meal from Sippi featuring heaping plates of fried shrimp and speckled sea trout, along with thick slices of warm, butter-melting, home-baked bread, we were on our way back north.

CHAPTER TWENTY-TWO

Timber Time

I first met the Reverend Jim Beck in a backroads café in North Dakota. Introduced by a mutual friend, conversation during our impromptu lunch time get-together revolved around ... what else ... wildfowling. Jim, a good 15 years my junior, was anything but subdued when it came to throwing in his two cents worth. "If his sermons are only half as high powered as his obvious exuberance when it comes to talking about our sport," I thought, "they must really be something special." After a protracted, two-hour bull session we parted company amiably enough, but still little more than like-minded strangers.

That's why I was more than a little taken aback when, a couple years later, quite out of the blue, my phone rang and I found the good reverend on the other end. After barely a minute of small talk, he, as is his style, got right to the point, asking me if I wanted to tag along on a little Arkansas duck hunting jaunt he was planning for that January. Explaining that the setup simply involved freelancing some public flooded green timber in northeast Arkansas with several new acquaintances of his, I couldn't think why not. So I probably surprised him a little by promptly answering in the affirmative.

I had no clue what I was getting myself into but I reasoned that as long as his BOSS was looking over our shoulders, we couldn't go wrong. But then came the boat ride from hell.

Anyone who thinks waterfowling is not a risky business should've been with us that bone-chilling 15-degree morning. After meeting us at our motel in Jonesboro, Tommy Adams, there-to-fore only an e-mail and voice-on-the-phone acquaintance of Jim's, drove us to a boat landing on the St.

Francis River, WMA. There we hooked up with Shorty Jones, one of Tommy's hunting partners, and who we'd come to learn through simple observation, was pretty much his mentor.

Wasting no time, we slipped two 16-foot duck boats off their trailers and loaded up. My Lab, Tanner and I jumped in with Tommy, while Rev. Jim saddled up with Shorty. The "short man" took the point, cracking the throttle on his 25 horse-power Merc with his left hand while holding his million-candle-power spot aloft with his right. Tommy did the same, and the flat out rat race down the boat trail was on. I scrunched as low in the jon boat as I could, holding Tanner by the collar as Cypress knees flashed by the gunnels and Shorty ducked to dodge the occasional overhead branch. I was certain an icy plunge was imminent.

After 20 exhilarating, breathtaking minutes we finally pulled into "the hole." There the boys idled around the 70-yard gap in the flooded timber, breaking ice and adding three wing-spinners to the rig that already floated there. With water too deep to wade, we slid both boats into the brush and settled in to wait out the final 20 minutes to shooting time.

Everything was quiet save for the hooting of several owls. At first each of us was content to listen to the early morning sounds of the forest, while savoring the hopeful anticipation of the hunt to come. Then the banter began.

"Hey Tommy," Shorty called then asked, "how's your wife and my kids this mornin'?"

"Just fine, but they're still waitin' for ya'll to drop off the groceries you promised." Tommy coolly replied.

It struck me then just how this great sport of ours ... duck hunting ... often makes strange boat-fellows. I mean, there we were, two good 'ole boy, rebel Baptists, one unaffiliated Yankee minister, and another yank, myself, who subscribes solely to the Church Of The Great Outdoors. Yet we were there together, inexplicably bound by the common thread that is the love of our game.

The battle of guidespeak continued, and I was all ears, until whistling wings overhead abruptly announced the approach of legal shooting time. As if someone had flipped a switch, the mood turned deadly serious. And nothing underscored that point more than the sight of the reverend. While the rest of us were bundled up for all we were worth, there sat Jim, stripped down to a turtleneck and a flannel shirt. No way was he going to let bulky clothes impede his gunswing!

There was precious little shooting light in the swamp when that first mallard materialized fluttering through the trees. A three-gun salute splashed the greenhead and Tanner was off, breaking ice and struggling through the viney, submerged underbrush on his first ever deep woods retrieve. There was no time to savor the dogwork because just as he clamped down on his prize, a flock of nearly 50 birds began to succumb to Tommy and Shorty's aggressive calling. After two wide swings the ducks totally committed, tumbling from the brightening sky like so many leaves from a tree. The mallards were strung out, some still hanging in the tree-tops, while others backpedaled right in our face. When Shorty commanded, "Cut'em!" we did, dropping the six closest drakes cleanly.

It was only then that I realized Shorty had yet to reach for his gun. "Is he just being polite?" I wondered. "Or is he testing us, the northern strangers that we still were?"

After completing his multiple retrieves, again, under Shorty's watchful eye, Tanner clamored aboard with the last duck firmly clasped in his maw, and promptly showered Tommy and I with an icy spray. The yellow dog shivered uncontrollably as his coat and vest quickly glazed over with its own skim of ice. Slipping my hand between his rib cage and the neoprene that covered it, I was glad to feel the warmth. In short order, with his head on a swivel watching birds flash high overhead, he was ready to go again.

And go he did, as the classic timber shoot, thanks to our new friends, continued. With Shorty finally joining in on the gunning, only two hours passed before our four-mallard limits had been reached.

We stopped for lunch that day in the small town of Truman. There, at the lunch counter of the local pharmacy and gossip exchange, we feasted on the BLTs and cheeseburgers Shorty had bragged about all morning. Great chow aside, what impressed me most was the waterfowl-oriented culture in general, and the sincere friendliness of the people in particular. From the waitress to the pharmacist, on up to the business types, everyone spoke the common language that is duck hunting. "Ya'll been killin' any?" was the question sure to begin every conversation.

Now, judging by our accents ... or the lack thereof ... it was obvious to all that we weren't locals. So, when I ordered a doggy-bagged burger to go for Tanner, I got a curious look to be sure. But when I noted that on our four-man, only $14 bill there was a No-Charge for the dog's burger, I couldn't believe it. Questioning her, the 'ole gal at the cash register just smiled and winked saying, "Aw honey, we're kinda' fond of our duck dogs too!"

After a nap and a dinner of Jim's barbecued duck breast rollups, the evening's sleep came fitfully. Had the morning's hunt been too good to be true? Could we be in for a repeat? Would that 4 a.m. wakeup call ever come?

That second day our crew was three boats strong, as we were joined by Tommy and Shorty's buddy, Jason "Taterhead" Taylor. With a reputation for wild boat driving and wrecking, Shorty made sure Tater brought up the rear in our high-speed, pre-dawn parade.

Hunting a bigger, shallower hole, we were able to slip out of the boats and assume the classic tree-hugging position, stationing Tanner on a tree stand. After taking a handful of early birds, the morning flight slowed to a trickle. As it did the gnawing, grinding cold began to seep in. After an hour in the literally ice cold water first Tanner and I, then finally Jim, took refuge in one of the boats.

Tater spotted 'em first, a nosebleed high flock of mallards ... mere specks in the deep blue sky ... winging our way from the south. I couldn't believe they were worth the effort but first Tater, then Tommy and Shorty tore into 'em with a series of highballs, the likes of which I'd never heard. Amazingly, the birds broke formation and began to look.

Keeping our heads down, the show began to unfold as round and round the mallards went, each pass just a tad lower than that before. Calling at the birds' wingtips and tails, the three duckmen blew their brains out. And the educated, late-season ducks responded, but ever so tentatively. Minutes passed like hours. But finally the whirling mass of mallards ... surely 300 strong ... was just above the treetops, temptingly, well within gun range.

When a group of six hens finally "did it," plopping into the decoys, Jim made a move, attempting to stand to shoot. I grabbed him by the shoulder ... much to his surprise ... and yanked him back down. No one had made the call. I peeked at Tater then, and he at me, shaking his head in the negative even as he continued to call and work the birds.

I sensed this was something special. If the boys could land the majority of these birds they'd win their game, the ultimate game, irrespective of any shooting.

Then, out of nowhere, a flock of greenwings probably 20 birds strong, darted low though the trees to lightly splash down directly in front of Jim and I. Again the hair-triggered reverend flinched. And again I jerked him back down. But when I did the teal flushed, sending the wrong message to the mallards above.

Just that fast the sky emptied. Not a shot had been fired. But be there no doubt, a lasting memory had been made. Jim might have been a little distraught, but Jason, Shorty, and Tommy were grinnin' from ear to ear.

"Now that's what I'm talkin' about!" Shorty uncharacteristically effused. To which I countered, "I get it short man. I get it."

We ended that morning's hunt well short of a limit. But when I shook Shorty's hand back at the ramp and simply thanked him for a great time, I could tell he knew I meant it. When he in turn offered to split a Moonpie, a cheap local confection he always packed along, as he'd say, "Just to keep my energy up," I knew we'd finally passed muster.

We enjoyed a number of great hunts with the boys after that wonderful day. Some were productive in terms of birds, some not. But it was valued time spent with like-minded friends, all.

Sure love it when a plan comes together, even if on my part, there wasn't one. Thanks for calling, Jim.

CHAPTER TWENTY-THREE

Spring Snows...
The Mud,
The Blood, and
The Gear

*T*hanks *to some progressive thinking, the U.S. and Canadian powers that be proposed and implemented a spring season on light geese in the mid-'90s. A seemingly drastic measure, it was the best tool, we were told, with which to try to stem the tide that was a mid-continent light goose population running wild and out of control. A population that had exploded to the point where it seriously threatened the long term well being of its ever-fragile sub-arctic, and arctic breeding grounds.*

Hunters needed to step up to the plate. With a rallying cry of "Save The Tundra," a lot of us were thrilled by the opportunity to do just that. And so the spring snow goose wars began. Armed with unplugged guns and electronic calls, little did we expect early on, that the "enemy" would handily win more battles than not.

When the phone rang in late April I was a little surprised to hear John Devries on the other end. After all, whenever he calls the essence of our conversation revolves around getting together to "chase some fowl," as he commonly refers to our often spontaneous adventures. Even though I was

thinking early season fishing at the time, it was John's talk of giving the spring snow geese one last go that soon had my ear.

John was uncharacteristically cautious as he spoke of locating several good-sized roosts of late-migrating, mostly juvenile snows hugging the SoDak/NoDak border. "Now these flocks are running only 500, to at most 1,500 birds. There are no massive tornadoes like we've seen during a million-bird push in March," John was quick to point out before he added, "They look happy though, and no one's been messin' with 'em. If they hang around and conditions hold, we could put a real whupin' on 'em!

Well, that's all it took. Knowing John never says what he doesn't mean, I was in.

With snowflakes flickering in the headlights we struck out early that MAY morning. As we drove John spoke gleefully of the winter-like forecast calling for plummeting temps, building winds, and three or four inches of snow. Knowing how "pleasant" it is to lie out in that stuff, I can't say I fully shared his enthusiasm.

Arriving at the field we joined his buddies, Al and Bubba, and began hustling gear and decoys. With John's innovatively rigged four wheeler and its trailer, we were able to get everything and everyone out to the muddy sunflower stubblefield in just two trips. It was still dark when we completed the elaborate set of 150 full bodies and a like number of silhouettes. Our early work done, we hunkered down to greet the grudgingly dawning day.

With Al and his dog, Max, on one end, and my Lab, Tanner, and I on the other, we layed out in a line just inside the downwind edge of the spread. As gray daylight oozed through the low scud the wind began to kick, and the snow, flying sideways, began to thicken.

Shooting time came and went. And the sky brightened, at least as much as it was going to on that dreary spring day. With the cold and damp settling into my bones, and with more than an hour of not so much as seeing or hearing a goose, I began to think, "Damn! The 'wild one' has snookered us again." But then finally, there it was, the sweet sound of distance-filtered goose music.

With the e-callers playing their seductive songs, and after seconds that seemed like minutes, the day's first birds simply materialized amid the driving snowflakes. The flock ... probably 20 geese strong ... hovered on tightly bowed wings only 30 to 70 yards high. When the wind pushed them over us John barked the order. In no time Max and Tanner had our first five snows ... a great start ... all piled up.

The birds were on the move then, and we had no time to celebrate. Coming from two different roost ponds, it seemed every goose in the vicinity wanted breakfast. And the real good news was we were set up exactly where they expected to find it. It was time to get down to business. And conduct business we did!

Our stars were aligned that day. With the combination of snotty weather and young birds operating without the benefit of adult supervision, we quickly depleted our ammo.

That glorious morning proved one for our record books. The heat of the battle displaced all sensation of wet and cold as flock after small, naïve, workable flock sucked to the spread. And though, like always, there was room for improvement, everyone shot pretty well. Doubles were common, and before the shoot was over, everyone had scored at least one clean triple. And the dogs, Max and Tanner, both youngsters, happily retrieved themselves to near exhaustion.

After three-and-a-half hours of the most electrifying wildfowling a man and dog could ever hope to encounter, the flight eventually petered out. Our efforts, incredibly, had taken their toll to the tune of 112 geese, a mixture of snows, blues, and Ross'.

That hunt was a far cry from my first with John several years earlier.

It was March of 1997 when I first met up with John and his partner at the time, Mike Schell, in southeastern Nebraska. A friend and I had booked a couple days with the two mobile, spring time-transient, but otherwise North Dakota home-based snow goose guides, as our introduction to the spring hunt.

Meeting up with the long-faced pair in their motel room, it was obvious something was amiss.

"Well," Mike began glumly. "We've got good news and bad news for you guys. The good news is there's a ton of birds around. The bad news is we've just found out that in this zone hunting them is allowed only every other day, and weekends."

We were booked for a Tuesday and Wednesday, meaning that we'd get to hunt only Wednesday. The boys were falling-over-themselves, sincerely apologetic. So much so that they offered to pop for dinner that evening, over which we got to know them, especially John, pretty well.

It doesn't take much, we quickly realized, to get John going when the topic is white geese. Before we knew it, and right before our eyes, he morphed into one, his dark eyes all bugged out, his back arched, and his arms outstretched to imitate the bowed wings he no doubt wished they were. Then, rocking back and forth as if fighting a gusting headwind, he craned his neck forward with his head swiveling, all the time verbalizing what he thinks ... heck ... knows the geese are saying. You simply have to see and hear it to believe it. It's a performance that is at once sincere and mesmerizing.

If for no other reason, just making Mike and John's acquaintance, I felt even then, made the trip worthwhile. It has certainly proved to be the case.

So we spent that first day cruisin' the Rainwater Basin ... an area I'd never seen before ... marveling at and photographing that year's vanguard of the spring migration of 'fowl. Just being among the ducks, the clouds of mallards, swirling fights of long-necked, fully sprigged pintails, and ponds plastered with the full gamut of divers, all in their brightest courtship colors, warmed my heart. But it was the geese, as always, that stirred my hunter's soul. Specklebillies in numbers I never knew existed dotted the thawing fields, and massive tornado-like clouds of snows, rolled smoke-like over the countryside in every direction. It's an oversimplification to say I'd never seen anything like it.

We had only the next day to hunt, but with the numbers of geese in evidence, "Surely," I thought, "It'll be a good one."

Well, it was good, and long, and unproductive.

Setting up in the still black of night we deployed a beautiful rig of brand new full bodies numbering 240 strong. Never had I had a part in setting such a lifelike spread. Situated in a high and dry winter wheat field, we were a scant half-mile from what the boys had determined to be a major roost pond. But it was one that was oddly silent that calm, still, star-studded morning.

A brilliant sunrise eventually flooded our field but the cloudless skies remained devoid of geese. John got restless, went to his truck, and checked out the roost which proved, as we suspected, to be empty.

"They were there yesterday afternoon," he explained to Mike who only shook his head in disgust and replied, "Damn it!" They must have pulled out over night."

What to do? Pull it? Look for different birds? Set up somewhere else? Or wait it out? It was quite a dilemma. But then the geese helped make up our minds.

A southerly breeze had began to puff, and on it rode the day's first snows, birds flying so high that though we could hear them, we could barely pick them out without binoculars. But seeing something they liked, those first strato-sailing flocks started to loosely funnel earthward, eventually lighting, ever so gently, on our nearby pond. As the wind picked up so did the intensity of the flight, as flock after migrating flock fell, like so many giant snowflakes, eventually paving the pond all but a solid white.

It was quite the show. One that passed the time and offered the potential of an evening shoot, should the travel-weary birds come off to feed.

But, as our luck would have it, they didn't. That first, much-anticipated spring hunt ended without any of us firing a shot. "The enemy won the battle today," John announced with a sobering finality. "But our time will come."

And true to his prophetic words, it has, time and again. Seeing the potential that first, abbreviated trip, I've chased around with John every spring since. Whether to Nebraska, South Dakota, or North Dakota ... wherever we needed to go ... we went. We've had a few great shoots. And we've had a number of good ones. Yet more than any, we've had plenty that were neither. But that, we've all learned, is the reality of spring snow goose HUNTING.

Almost always a lot of work, and often as not totally frustrating, when it works ... well ... there's really nothing like winning a battle with "whitey." And even when you lose, just the awesome sights and sounds of the hunt can leave an everlasting impression. Such was the case when my son Billy, a couple buddies, and myself caught up with John one spring in eastern SoDak, a few years after we'd first met.

John greeted us enthusiastically to say the least.

"Things look great for the morning guys," he piped up immediately. "Our quarter section field was covered up this afternoon. I don't want to jinx us, but it sure looks like we couldn't be in better shape."

For John-boy to be so psyched, I knew we were in for something special.

The mid-March morning dawned clear and bright, with only the slightest hope of a breeze. Classic bluebird conditions, the unfavorable type I always seem to encounter when I've got snow geese on the brain.

But just as the eyeball-burning sun popped over the gently sloping eastern edge of the otherwise platter-flat 160 acres of South Dakota corn stubble, the distant barking of the day's first flights of snows filtered over the countryside. Within minutes it became apparent that John's homework had paid off, as major flocks of geese began to stream to our field, seemingly from every point on the compass.

Now, as an enthusiast, I'd hunted the white goose all across prairie Canada, and up and down the Central Flyway for more than 25 years by that time. And though I'd always thrilled to the spectacle that is commonly referred to as "the white tornado," I'd always wondered what it would be like to be directly under one. I was about to find out as the milling geese began to build into a spiraling vortex directly above us.

It was like lying at the bottom of a blender and looking up to see flock after wavering flock of snows and blues join the swelling, swirling mass. We were under a sensory overload if there ever was one. With thousands ... no, tens of thousands ... of geese circling, weaving, and whiffling overhead, I found it nearly impossible to focus. I could no more concentrate on a single bird than I could a solitary mosquito in a swarm.

I'd guess the closest geese had kited down to within 70 or 80 yards. With layer upon spinning layer of birds stacked above, the tornado easily topped out at 300 yards or more.

Then there was the sound. At first it was the building, visceral crescendo of so many wildly vocal birds. Then the strange and eery sensation that was their calls being muted, if not totally drowned out, by the turbine-like roar of so many strong wings ripping at moist, heavy air.

Just being there, with my knees visually shaking, straining to steady my quivering young hound, Tanner, who I had throttled between them, was every bit as much as any, the thrill of a wildfowling lifetime. Yet I had to guard against drop-jawed amazement. Better to keep my mouth shut, as goose turds pelted down like a hailstorm.

Nothing so magnificent lasts very long, and neither did this spectacle. I was never seriously tempted to even reach for my gun. With so many geese, so many eyes, and so many years of collective experience in dealing with decoy spreads, it was only a matter of time before our jig was up. Once we were made, it seemed only seconds and the geese ... all of them ... were gone,

vanished, as if into thin air. The sudden tranquility was surreal ... "Had it really happened? Were they really there? Or had it all been just a dream?"

It had long been my contention that it's the snow goose ... the wild one, the white devil, whitey, the enemy, or whatever you want to affectionately label him ... that truly puts the Spectacle in Spectacular. Anyone who had been there that once-in-a-lifetime, awe-inspiring morning, could never argue my point.

We didn't kill any geese that day, but to a man, we agreed it didn't matter.

CHAPTER TWENTY-FOUR

Potholin'... Again

The spring snow goose hunt wasn't the only good thing on the waterfowl front in the mid-to-late '90s. There was great news in that the water had returned to the prairies. Water that filled the permanent ponds and lakes to overflowing. And water that, more importantly, left the prairie pothole region pockmarked with a myriad of temporary, but oh so fertile wetlands. The natural phenomena spawned not only ducks, but a whole new generation of duck hunters. Something I witnessed firsthand when Steve Loebaka invited me to join his buddy Eric Benin and himself on a NoDak potholin' trip. It was the first time in a lifetime that I wasn't "in charge" of the hunt. And that felt odd. But I knew my place, and was happy to just tag along. Though I'll admit I had a hard time keeping my mouth shut that first morning.

Grinding to a halt at the rough two-track's dead end, we watched as the still dark, but overcast and featureless night sky unexpectedly came alive with the grandest of lightning displays. Then listened to the still distant thunder as it rolled across the prairie. Fully expecting to wait it out, I was silently amazed to see Eric jump out from behind the wheel and start gearing up. Steve, ever-the-good-soldier, promptly followed suit. As did I, realizing I had little choice.

The two wide-eyed enthusiasts, both all of 20 years my junior, knew full well what I was thinking. (ie. Ducks never fly in a thunderstorm!) But they ... rightly, I suppose ... didn't care. So we saddled up. Both of them, running on adrenaline, athletically toted heavy sacks of decoys, while I, suddenly realizing I'd become the "old man" they enjoyed referring to me as, stumbled along behind. My Lab, Sadie, bounced happily ahead of us as we marched, not unlike the Three Stooges, headlong in the direction of the fast-approaching storm.

Shamus

We worked to set the rig on the crescent-shaped pothole as dim, gray day-light oozed into our surroundings. No sooner had we taken up our positions in the cattailed fringe than, after a flashbulb-bright strobe that lit up our world, accompanied by a howitzer-like shot of thunder, the skies opened up. There we stood, our heads ducked and our GORE-TEX'd backs to the sheet-ing, gale-driven-sideways downpour. If there ever was a scene that depicted our sport as little more than big boys playing outside, (which in essence, is really all our time spent fishing and hunting is) I've never seen it.

I wanted, in the worst way, to say it. To state the obvious. To say, "I told you so." The boys knew I wanted to. And I knew they knew. But I didn't utter a word. When I finally glanced their way I could see the pair grin-nin', causing first me, then both of them to laugh out loud. It was a child-like moment to be sure. And I realized then, by keeping my mouth shut, I'd passed their unplanned test.

As soon as the storm blew itself out the birds started to fly, and better yet, work our spread. Taking them as they came, professing no stodgy preference for one glamour duck or another, we enjoyed a classic pothole shoot that produced no less than 14 different species, a mixture of divers and puddlers, in our 18 bird bag.

It was a great start to a wonderful trip that produced quality hunt after simple, quality pothole hunt. We got along fine, had a great time, and at week's end, vowed to do it all again. Which we did for a couple more years.

And we weren't alone. A whole new generation of duck hunters, those of Steve and Eric's vintage, came to the prairie to experience it's incomparable hunting ... hunting like I'd first experienced 20 years earlier ... during this timely wet period.

But there was trouble brewing on the horizon. Mother nature turned the faucet off by the late '90s. While the promotion of NoDak waterfowling, in print and on video, continued; the all-productive temporary wetlands once again receded, and duck populations declined, amid still-growing hunting pressure, (everybody and his duck hunting brother had rushed to NoDak). The result being a major degradation in the quality of the wildfowling the Roughrider State offered.

It's only human nature to want too much of a good thing. But we learned there is a steep price to pay in its pursuit when it comes to NoDak's ducks. We learned ... or at least should have ... that too much unregulated hunting pressure is simply not a good thing.

CHAPTER TWENTY-FIVE

Oh Canada

With the hunting in North Dakota no longer what it used to be, I turned to my prairie hunting roots and began to once again look northward, to Canada, in an effort to find my quality hunting Holy Grail. A lot of water had run under my wildfowling bridge by the late '90s and it had been nearly 30 years since I'd first hunted prairie Canada. I'd aged. I'd become, in my 50s, at least somewhat of an old timer. And time, quite honestly, had become more important to me than money. While nothing beats the satisfaction of freelancing, I was no longer willing to devote the windshield time it takes to be successful at it. To that end I began to search for guides/outfitters who could expedite the process of putting me into the birds that I wanted to hunt without their supervision. It was and remains an ongoing process that has provided many a rewarding hunt in locales all across Canada. But more importantly, it has generated a network of new, like-minded friends. None of which has been more special than Randy Lewis of Brandon, Manitoba. The hunting he's helped me and my buddies enjoy has been nothing short of phenomenal.

Our first-ever hunt with Randy was in a field of burnt wheat stubble. Its toasted waste grain proving the attraction for a good number of snows and blues as well as a wealth of ducks. As the just-turned, golden leaves in the popple-laced bush that surrounded our field came alive, flickering in the freshening breeze, they provided a striking contrast to the cloudless, robin egg-colored sky. A sky that, in brightening daylight, was soon etched with flights of fowl, both hungry, low-winging locals, and high-riding migrants.

Steve Loebaka and Tracy Messner guarded one side of the spread. My son Billy and I, along with my year-and-a-half-old yellow pup, Tanner, held down the other. We weren't covered up with birds by any means. But the flight was steady as we tried ... for some unknown reason that occasionally accounts for poor shooting ... not so successfully to make the most of every opportunity, be it with the ducks or the geese. In the end we'd taken 18 snows and blues and a dozen ducks among us. More than enough to classify it as a grand shoot. But the best part was we didn't hear a shot, other than ours, all morning. We were the only hunters on that part of the prairie. And it was a beautiful thing.

While that hunt met ... hell, far exceeded ... our expectations, little did we realize just how "average,"(and I don't mean that in a derogatory sense), it was. It's just that wildfowling on the Canadian prairie can be, unbelievably, worlds better. A hunt with Randy's crew five years after that first one, serves to make my point.

Travis Cairns, one of Randy's longtime sidekicks strode up to my truck at o-dark thirty that morning and announced, with bright-eyed enthusiasm that belied his many successive, sleep-deprived days of guiding, "Follow me boys!" When the young man speaks in such an emphatic tone, I've learned it's a good, a very good thing.

As if we'd been slapped in the face, we were suddenly wide awake and off to the races. Our mad dash through the prairie night ending at yet another field of wheat-stubbled dreams. While we hustled to set the rig Travis spoke enthusiastically of the ducks, snows, and Canadas that were using the field. One that had yet to be hunted all season. "The ducks'll come from the ponds in the bush on the north edge of the field boys. The snows are roosting on a lake a mile and a half west. The Canadas ... cacklers for the most part ... are roosting barely a mile east, eh? Keep a sharp eye. You should do well."

Now, we're not the types to count our birds until they're bagged. But, with geese barking in the distance and ducks happily gabbling away while they thrashed the still-dark skies overhead, it was awful hard to contain our enthusiasm as we got situated in our low-profile blinds.

The shoot that ensued passed in a blur of mind-boggling action. Coming under virtual attack at first light, I, due to no more than graying seniority, was assigned the task of calling the shot. And a gut-wrenching job it was. Our first priority, it was agreed by all, was the geese. But the ducks just wouldn't leave us alone. They were always there, wave after persistent wave; constantly in the peripheral distance, but often right in our face. The mallards, along with a few pintails, persistently kamikazeed the rig set in the exact spot, the "X" on the "X"; where they'd fed, according to Travis, for more than a week. Ducks or geese? Geese or ducks? Would it be better to wait out the snows wavering in low from the west? Or should we take the darks stringing our way from the east? I'd make the call, in a situation I finally realized in relief, which, thanks to the sheer number of birds, I could do no wrong.

Mike Lambrecht, Rick Rosenberg, Billy and I fought the good fight. Though a crisp, chilly morning, with a hint of the winter that was only weeks away in the air, we shot ourselves into a sweat in the effort to hold our ground. The result was no small amount of work for our happy-to-oblige canine partners: Sully, BB, Maggie, and Tanner.

When the battle ended that morning-of-mornings our generous limits of mallards and Canadas were complemented by no less than 68 snows! Even Travis, the ever quick-witted one, was at a loss for words. All he could mumble was "Geez boys I knew it'd be bloody good. But nothing like this, eh?"

That week in Manitoba, spent with good and like-minded friends, has become "the" mainstay of my wildfowling year. But I continue to wander all of prairie Canada, enjoying to the fullest, this magnificent land of boundless wildfowling opportunity.

From the shores of a tiny Lake Winnepegosis island where Tanner and I shivered and thrilled to the other-worldly, jet-like roar of massive rafts of redheads and cans taking wing. Only to witness, moments later and for hours to come, the birds' confident, relentless, even reckless attack, in bus load-sized flocks, (Our guide Russel McKay likened the 23- to 24-duck flocks to the capacity of the school buses used by students in his village), on our meager, well-worn diver rig. To the shooting gallery-like atmosphere that developed over the barely acre-sized watering hole that was a must-stop for each of the 3,000 or so mallards that came to gorge in the sloppily harvested 160-acre Saskatchewan pea field it centered, starting, for some strange reason, but just like clock work, at 3 p.m. each early October afternoon. And on up to the Peace River Country of Alberta where the prime wheat stubble and pea fields are paved with swarms of dark geese and ducks on a twice-daily basis. I continue to marvel at, and enjoy to the fullest, the awesome sights and sounds the Canadian prairie has to offer.

CHAPTER TWENTY-SIX

Seaduckin'

Sea duck hunting, on the ocean, with eiders being the primary quarry, had for me, always been the stuff of dreams. The romance of it all, the big water, the challenging environment, the boats, and the gear ... well ... it's enthralling.

When the time finally came to give it a shot, I was more than ready to pull the trigger on the adventure.

"Pitch in Heeah! Tip in Heeah!" Todd Jackson, our outfitter chanted aloud; talking to the line of wavetop-scraping "Eidahs" pumping our way into the freshening northerly breeze. Thanks to his surgically corrected 20/10, x-ray like vision, he announced, "There's three hens in front and one in the rear sandwiching two drakes. If they work, you know the drill."

By this time, our second morning of the hunt, we knew it darn well. We'd better let 'em come in, at least well over the decoy strings, and then gun the big white drakes only. We were only happy to oblige.

My first sea ducking trip to Maine was unfolding to be everything I'd anticipated and much more. Having done a ton of open water hunting on Lake Michigan through the years, I knew the basics when it came to stringing decoys and gunning from open boats. And I was familiar with the flight characteristics of sea ducks, oldsquaws and scoters in particular. But this North Atlantic, saltwatered adventure was proving special for several unexpected reasons.

The first of these was Todd himself. A young man, in his middle 30s, he exudes an unabashed love for what he does, and a day-in, day-out intensity that is remarkable given that he guides for sea ducks the better part of three grueling months each year. With license plates that read Eider, and a home on Eider Lane, his respect for the birds is obvious and exceptional.

He'll allow only high percentage shots, and then on drakes only, to be taken. If there's a cripple, no matter how strong the flight is, recovering the downed bird is, as it should be, job one.

Though Todd will gladly put his hunters on the birds of their choice, old-squaw (a.k.a. Longtail), the full variety of scoters, or eiders, it's the "Eidah" that's number one in his duck hunting heart. And he's so taken by his passion that his idea of vacation is to take a week off to gun sea ducks in Alaska. He's truly the type of young man we need to carry on our wildfowling heritage.

Then there's the sheer beauty of coastal Maine. Its highly irregular, spruce-studded, otherwise granite shores are a myriad of bays and islands, with each vista proving as pleasing to the eye as the last or the next. Annually producing its fair share, these constantly wind-worried waters come alive each autumn with even more migrating sea ducks, the ever-spectacular eiders being the most prominent.

And it is the common eider, finally, that this sea ducking show is really all about. Nothing proved that point more than a barely minute-long episode during the final morning of our hunt.

An ugly, snotty, December morning it was. We arrived at the boat ramp still cloaked in the dark of night, only to be greeted by torrential rains driven sideways on the teeth of a 'noreasterly gale. I wouldn't have argued had Todd decided to call the whole thing off. Heck, as it was, I was ready to call in sick. But when Todd jumped out of his Suburban and began to suit up as if it was just another day, which I suppose for him it was, my hunting partners and I answered the bell, albeit somewhat reluctantly.

After the boatride-from-hell in the 20-foot TDB, the first gray light suggested to our collective surprise that the day would actually dawn. Rigging the decoys and anchoring up alongside the ledge was a battle, but one worth winning, on this it would prove, as this wild and woolly a sea ducking day as a hunter could ever hope to experience.

With full shooting light, such as it was, we found ourselves smack dab in the middle of a sea duck parade. Our first volley splashed three ponderously low-flying whitewing scoters. The next dumped the same number of fully

plumed drake ei-
ders. Then we managed
a perfect pair of long-tailed
drake oldsquaws, before the eiders, string after downwind string,
really began to work us over.

We were one bird shy of our limit,
my last, when that "trophy" moment occurred. Through rain-splattered glasses I
watched intently as that solitary drake ... a
dead duck flying if there ever was one ... pitched in
low over the stern line of decoys. In an otherwise world of muted grays
and dim fuzzy edges, the big, strikingly white bird seemed aglow, center-
focused in my mind's eye. He hung there, fighting the gusty headwind,
stubbly wings pumping, his neck craning downward not unlike a decoying goose, all but stalled out. As he did an exceptionally tall roller crashed
on the suddenly tide-exposed ledge below him, sending a geyser of salt
spray skyward. Flaring vertically, but only momentarily to avoid a dous-
ing, this grand duck of the sea then plopped, ever-so-casually, into the rig.
The bird's ability to handle ... heck ... apparently revel in the rough and
tumble conditions, made a statement, seeming to say, "Hey, this is my
kinda' day!"

Immersed in the show, I hadn't even considered shooting. That it
proved a clear case of "free in, free out" seemed only appropriate. I
watched him wing off thinking that with luck, the gaudy drake and his
offspring will grace Maine's coast well beyond my lifetime's memory of
his splendor and sea-going style.

CHAPTER TWENTY-SEVEN

Down Mexico Way

*R*everend Jim's offer to join him on a trip to Old Mexico's province of Tamaulipas was finally too tempting. "We'll shoot redheads on the Laguna Madre and pintails, along with some smaller ducks, on the fresh water ponds inland," he effused.

Sure sounded interesting. But I was torn. My impression of Mexican waterfowling was that it amounted to just what Jim called it: shooting ... unlimited shooting ... not hunting. The "sports" who participated in the endeavor apparently had no qualms about pounding out big bags, justifying their actions by the simple greedy fact that they had paid the big bucks to do it.

Now, I like to shoot as much as anyone. And I can understand a more liberal bag limit in locales, such as those in Mexico, where hunting pressure and total kill, in terms relative to that of the States, is actually next to non-existent. But I can't understand how gunners ... and that's really all they are ... can treat ducks, a precious North American resource, with such a lack of respect that they are relegated to little more than targets. It's a sad fact, but two-man bags of 80-plus redheads or pintails, though not an every day occurrence, do commonly happen in Mexico.

Still, Mexican duck "hunting," was something I wanted to experience. By packing ethics, along with the rest of my gear, I was confident it would be a good experience. And it was.

One of my most memorable Mexican hunts was my first ever on the Laguna. Jim, 'ole Bob — a squat, well-bellied, thickly eye-glassed gentleman well into his 70s who was on his hunt of a lifetime — and I had just gotten situated in our simple brush and bench blind, strategically placed on a shallow eelgrass flat, when we first heard the big straight-piped airboat at work off in the distance. Only minutes later there arose a slow rolling

cloud of smoke on the horizon. At first it strung low, but then abruptly built, tornado-like, into a rising funnel shape that spun off trailing, seemingly evaporating puffs and wisps.

"That's one heck of a bunch of redheads," Jim, who'd been to this dance before, offered excitedly. Then added, "Keep a sharp eye, some will surely be here soon."

"Where? I can't see 'em. What you lookin' at?" Bob questioned, a sense of urgency in his crackling voice.

Realizing that he was likely a little short on eyesight I countered, "Don't worry. If they get any closer you'll see 'em. I'll keep you posted."

Agreeing that seniority had honors, the plan was to give 'ole Bob first crack at any ducks that worked us.

I spotted them first, a good swarm of birds diving in from my right. "Here they come Bob. Get ready!"

"Where are they? I still can't find 'em!" he almost hyper-ventilated in response.

When he did finally get a visual on the then tight-swinging flock he commanded, suddenly taking charge as he tilted his face back down, "Don't look! Don't look!"

Then, in a picture perfect scene, the "patos" were on us, coasting into our setup on locked wings like so many fighter jets landing in formation. I let them come around the corner from my downwind end of the blind and when I knew we'd all get decent shooting, made the call.

"Oh Jeez! Oh Jeez!" Bob muttered as he struggled shakily to his feet, awkwardly fitting the well-worn 870 to his shoulder.

With the sun at our backs it was easy to pick "color" and when the smoke cleared five fat "Roho Cabesa" (red head) drakes floated belly up.

"I tripled! I tripled!" the old timer claimed with a shit-eatin' grin. I looked at Jim and he at me, waiting for the old fart to come clean. But he didn't. Not knowing what to say, we didn't say a thing. I was certain I'd dropped a pair of tail-enders. And Jim later told me he'd center-punched two, and maybe three, from the leading edge of the flock. Which I would have expected of him.

But 'ole Bob just kept goin' on and on.

"Wasn't that just wonderful boys? Just wonderful?" he chirped.

What were we to do but agree? He had us just where he wanted us, and took full advantage of the situation. To this day I'm not sure if Bob really believed he tripled or, if being the wiley old coot that he was, he pulled one over on us just because he could. Whatever the case, more power to him.

Every bit as special as the redheads of the Laguna Madre are its pintails. Which are commonly hunted on inland, freshwater ponds where the birds go to drink and desalinate.

Now, I'd taken my share of pintails over the years, but they were always incidental to other ducks. And I'd killed a few trophy-quality, fully sprigged drakes in the late season. But I'd never been on a pintail hunt of the type that allowed for drakes-only gunning should a hunter so choose. So when our outfitter spoke of the hunt he had planned for us the next morning, one where two of his clients several weeks earlier had piled up more than 120 birds, we were all ears.

As we sloshed our way to the simple sugar cane-sided blinds that morning, the darkness could not hide the blood in my gunning partners eyes. If a big shoot was in the offing, they were fully prepared, and intending to take advantage of it.

The hunt started out like gang busters. From first light on through the initial hour and a half the place was abuzz with pintails. In the relative gloom of pre-dawn they'd bore confidently in, twisting, turning, and swooping ever so gracefully, as only those long-necked ducks can. Even with the poor shooting light we could still find the long-spiked drakes as they flared in black silhouette against the gray sky.

As the day grudgingly brightened small flocks of ever-warier pintails, and the occasional surprise darting flight of teal, kept us on our toes. But come full daylight the big, obviously pressured birds, had our number. They'd circle at strato heights and work ever-so-cautiously, sometimes for five minutes or more, before, not wanting to get their sprigs shot off, they'd cancel their flight plan and wing off to find an alternate, unmanned watering hole.

It proved a fine, satisfying, but short hunt, producing, if not a bonanza, several taxidermy-worthy drakes for each gun. A noteworthy fact in that nowhere else in North American can this legally be done.

So, yeah, while poor sportsmanship does regularly rear its ugly head in Mexico, it doesn't mean there aren't unique and wonderful experiences to be had there. Like all hunting should be, it's what YOU make of it that matters most.

CHAPTER TWENTY-EIGHT

Alberta Calling

I'm nothing if not a student of the game. I read, watch, and listen to everything and anything I can pertaining to the world of wildfowling. Always have. And probably always will. In that endeavor I became well aware of Alberta and the fabulous hunting, particularly for dark geese, that it had to offer.

But Alberta ... even its central prairie country, and certainly the more renowned Peace River Country to the north, where the last vestige of the prairie butts up against the boreal forest ... is a long ways from anywhere. And it's certainly farther than my gang has the time or resources to go.

So, for the longest time, Alberta waterfowling had remained on my wish list. It seemed about as likely to happen as becoming an overnight success at this business of freelance outdoor writing — something I've been plugging away at for 30 years. But it was the writing, finally, that got me Alberta-bound.

Now, freelancing is hardly a lucrative avocation. And if you're going to make a living at it, (which I'm not), you're going to have to be both highly prolific, and willing to accept a subpar standard of living. That said, it does have its perks. Like the offer I had from an editor friend to pinch hit for him on a Beretta/Realtree- sponsored hunt with Sean Mann in central Alberta, all expenses paid. I was on it.

Sean Mann is one of those few truly full-time professional waterfowler-types. Parlaying a world championship goose calling title into a career, he makes his living by manufacturing and selling his own line of goose and duck calls, along with guiding/outfitting in both Alberta and his home turf of Maryland.

At least as far as I was concerned, his reputation preceded him. And he didn't disappoint.

Clean shaven and articulate, Sean would sooner pass as an investment banker than a waterfowl guide. And he runs a hunt from the perspective of the president and CEO I suppose he is. Every bit the field general, he commands your attention right from the get go. You could be the president of a multi-billion dollar company yourself, but come time to set decoys you're just another lackey, as he sends you off, two by two, to set the rig of silhouettes with explicit instructions.

During the hunt it's more of the same. Your job one is that of a shooter. You better keep your head down and don't move, or there will be hell to pay in the form of biting, sarcastic criticism.

The hunt is Sean's show. The field is his stage. And the birds, more than you the hunter, are his audience.

The man can blow a call! His virtuoso performances are almost musical as he works the birds, talking to them in intimate, but obviously understandable notes. Yet, while the calling sequences, as entertaining as they are, keep Sean center stage, and no doubt contribute in good part to the hunt's success, they are no way totally responsible for it.

It became readily apparent that Alberta is God's country when it comes to wildfowling. The part of its rolling prairie where Sean operates hosts migrating fowl in numbers hard to imagine. With the next-to-nonexistent hunting pressure, the naïve birds, it appeared to me, were made to work. Only after patterning them on a feed field (usually peas) for several days, and comfortable in the knowledge that he'd be working with thousands, not just hundreds of birds, would Sean hunt them. Yeah, the flagging and calling were factors, but on our hunts ... and they were truly spectacular ... it would have been difficult to keep the birds out of our setup in their field. More than anything Alberta produced our birds.

But that's not to sell Sean short. Even more than the technical excellence of his calling, it is his ability to read the birds, to know what they want to hear, and how they'd react, that impresses me most. Oddly enough, it was a go 'round with a flock of mallards a couple hundred birds strong that stands out in my mind.

Our first customers that glorious autumn morning were lessers and cacklers, the birds that had been scouted. But the smoke-like cloud of ducks that came rolling low over the distant knob in the field caught us by surprise. Spitting out his goose call Sean puckered up to his duck call and got right down to business. The mallards liked what they heard and were on us in a flash. But they didn't want to finish. We were forced to hold our fire while round and round they went, as mallards so often temptingly do, looking hard, but not committing. I thought for sure he'd call the shot when at last, the birds pitched straight in on locked wings, their bright orange feet paddling the air. But at 40 yards out they caught themselves again, flaring wildly to turn on a downwind rush that I thought would take them outa' town for good. It was then that Sean, between notes, piped up. "OK boys, we got 'em. When they swing this time they'll cruise right into our laps." I couldn't believe what I was hearing, and would've bet the bank to the contrary. But then there they were, hanging right in our faces.

The shooting was an afterthought. And we made the most of it. But it's

Sean's confidence and his truly exceptional knowledge of the birds, that I'll always remember most.

It was but a couple years later that I found myself Alberta-bound once again, this time to its famed Peace River Country. Blue Sky Outfitters, or more specifically its head man, Kevin McNeil was interested in hosting a writer-type in hopes, but without guarantee, that he'd get some print media exposure for his still fledgling operation. It was my good fortune to be tabbed the man for the job.

I first met up with Kevin one beautiful, late September afternoon in his hometown of McClennan. Suggesting I join him for the evening scout, I jumped at the chance to share a get-to-know-each-other cruise.

Kevin, I sensed, was particularly anxious for me to witness the evening flights off Kimiwan Lake. Materializing during the last hour of light, small strings of dark geese were soon in evidence, winging low and comfortable over the long-harvested grainfields. It was a grand show to be sure. But if the sheer volume of birds was to be the sole criteria, it really couldn't compare to that which might come off a major snow goose roost, or even a major stateside refuge like the Horicon Marsh.

"Look at these ones," Kevin would say, excitedly pointing to a larger hundred-bird flock. "Or how about those ones over there!," directing our focus to a flock touching down a mile distant. There was no doubt he was proud of what he had to offer. And all I knew at that point was, that that was good.

With the sun about to give up the ghost we came upon a quarter section of wheat stubble speckled with flocks of small Canadas, perhaps 500 birds in all. After studying the happy birds for a few minutes Kevin asked, "What say you and I give this field a go in the morning?" "You're the doctor. Looks good to me," I replied cooperatively, keeping my doubts to myself. Had they been big Canadas I'd not have had a problem. But I'd had way too many blowouts with similar scenarios involving the far warier small darks.

It was a quick and easy setup the next morning. After deploying a rig of approximately 80 silhouettes we simply surrounded our two layout blinds with a dozen Big Foot full bodies and settled in for the wait. We couldn't even stubble the blinds. There wasn't enough chaff to do so in the almost sterile, short-clipped field. Though textbook, our "X"-shaped rig appeared anything but impressive.

And that's what it seemed that first flight of geese thought as well. Round and round that boisterous flock of a dozen or so cacklers went, always passing close, but behind us. We could have sat up and turned to take the shot, but Kevin didn't want to make that move. And I was glad. Instead, he patiently worked with the call. Joining in when appropriate, I couldn't help but think, "Sean Mann we ain't!"

After what seemed like an eternity the birds finally cruised by on a downwind rush to turn base-to-final, and slid right in. With their powerful wings backpedaling, audibly thumping the thick, damp air, and their black feet first ruddering, then reaching for the ground, Kevin calmly, almost politely, called "Take 'em." So I did, but rather ineptly, in a whiff-kill-whiff sequence.

I'd been stricken with a case of my lifelong, goose fever. And that was my excuse ... legitimate or not ... for poor shooting. But Kevin hadn't even fired. When I asked "Wassup?" he sheepishly replied, "I forgot to load my gun."

We had a good laugh, but couldn't enjoy the moment for long. There were more birds stringing our way. Each subsequent flight played the game. With the cobwebs gone I quickly had my eighth bird down, which Tanner promptly deposited on our pile. Kevin was one goose short when he suggested we call it a shoot. "If it doesn't matter to you Jack," he said, "when I get to hunt myself I like to leave a little seed."

What a refreshing perspective!

I gunned with Kevin for four days that first trip. And each hunt, whether it was for geese, ducks, or a combination, came off pretty much as planned. The explanation being, per Kevin, that "The birds are doing what they're supposed to do." And therein lies the key to Kevin's success. Oh, he knows how to hunt them alright. And he does his homework, scouting and securing permission. But he is usually blessed with an abundance of fresh, unhunted birds all season long.

Peace Country, I learned, is essentially a bottleneck in the migratory funnel for waterfowl originating in Alaska and the Northwest Territories. It's in Peace Country, the northernmost projection of the prairie, that these ducks and geese first stage, and effectively fuel up before continuing down the flyway. But they don't come en masse. Rather, they transition through Kevin's hunting grounds throughout September and October. With fresh birds constantly arriving and stale birds departing, Kevin's naturally unique situation allows him to hunt the same feed fields all season long; since the old birds effectively lead the new birds to them.

But even in such a perfect world of wildfowl Kevin can be thrown a curve. And that's what we experienced the next year.

I hunted with Kevin for six days on that trip and only once did we enjoy a grand slam goose shoot. Oh, we killed geese on every outing. But they were what I thought to be classically challenging. Kevin, totally frustrated by the situation, had another perspective. "These birds just aren't acting like they're supposed to!" he complained straight-faced, but almost comically I thought, given my lifelong, real waterfowl world experience.

The goose migration through Alberta that year, thanks to unseasonably mild weather in the far north, was totally atypical. The result was that Kevin had to hunt old birds repeatedly. In doing so he got a heavy dose of what the rest of us know as goose hunting reality.

Still, his hunters were hardly lacking for action. Turning to his always reliable Plan "B," Kevin focused on Peace Country ducks. And Peace Country does have ducks! Quite possibly like nowhere else. It really is common, I learned, to find yourself in a field that's feeding 10,000 pea-drunk mallards or more. Or if you prefer, hunkered on the edge of a beaver pond or dugout these gullible, never-before-been-gunned birds use for drinking water. The only problem with the shooting, in either case, is that ... if you don't pace yourself, don't savor the show one shot, one bird at a time ... it'll be over way too quickly. So quickly, that only an hour after the dreamlike hunt is over, you might find yourself wondering if it had actually happened, and perhaps a bit fearful that it hadn't!

It was yet another assignment that took me back to Alberta once more. This time to hunt with the boys from Marlin to help them test drive their newly imported line of scatterguns. While that was fine, for me it was all about the hunt. And a grand one it proved to be.

If hunting with Sean Mann was a well-orchestrated production. And gunning with Kevin McNeil was all about taking advantage of a very special set of circumstances that produced predictable, reliable sport. Then being hosted by Jeff Klotz and his Alberta Flyway Outfitters was about organization.

Enthusiastic and unpretentious, Jeff made no bones about the fact that what he had to offer centered solely around unpressured birds. "You can take your skill, your fancy calls, spinning-wing gadgets and precise decoy sets," he offered. "Give me fresh birds and put me where they want to be, and I'll give you a hunt like no other."

While hunting central Alberta, Jeff relies on himself and two other full-time scouts to locate concentrations of unpressured birds. They regularly put on 500-700 klicks per day each in that substantial effort. Any hot setups are GPS'd with a trail leading right from the "X" in the field or on the pond edge, all the way back to camp. In a meeting each evening the options are weighed, and the guide is given the GPS unit that will lead him to the spot, sight unseen, the following morning. The whole process sounds pretty tactical. And it really is. But it works. As we happily found out during our stay.

Our group of five hunters included a couple of guys with some waterfowling experience. A rifleman on his first ever duck/goose hunt. A somewhat pompous, (and I'm being kind here), whiskey, wine, cigar, and gun writer from Beverly Hills. And me, the aging enthusiast living the dream of "Have Lab Will Travel." We were an interesting group to say the least.

While we were all expecting the type of slam bang goose shoot the Alberta prairies are famous for, it came as quite the surprise that ducks were on the schedule for that first morning. But what a hoot that hunt proved to be.

Come shooting light our pothole-laced barley field came under virtual attack by mallards swarming our way, low, but fast, with a stiff breeze on their tails, from roost water a mile east. Being newly acquainted, we kind of stumbled over ourselves trying to be polite at first. It was a comedy actually. "Take 'um!" someone would say. "Naw, YOU take 'em," would come the reply. The result, naturally, being that no one would. No one that is, until my "What the hell!" instincts prevailed, and I held back no longer. Soon everyone warmed to the task. And in the end a fine time was had by all.

After a mediocre afternoon goose hunt, hearing that the second morning's shoot would again be a ducky one, was music to our ears.

Deploying in low profile blinds along the edge of the only slough in another rolling, swathed barley field, we waited comfortably in the cool, pre-dawn darkness, as conversation easily flowed among the by then new friends.

The ducks were right on schedule. With the clock announcing it was time, and with just enough light to sharply silhouette the birds against the pinkening sky, they began to pour into our hole, scraping the hilltop to our north, then diving for the water ... their water ... for a drink before they fed. It was a pattern, our scout said, the ducks had been on for a week.

There was no holding back this morning. As the ducks ran the gamut our world became a shooting gallery. Birds crashed and splashed. Men babbled like little boys. And Tanner had a field day. Once, during the heat of the battle I heard our boy from California spout off, complaining, "Hey, your dog just ran right over me." "Yeah, so what's your point wine boy?" I responded in a tone that made everyone chuckle. 'Spose I could've gone easier on him, but I didn't have it in me.

Not long after sunrise we were done, eight-mallard limits each in hand. We could have drawn the hunt out, looking for drakes only in full daylight. But it would have been futile. This was the early season and the birds were far from colored out. To try to find a splash of green would have been far too frustrating for our newbies, who were having a tough enough time with their shooting as it was.

After that afternoon's goose hunt proved a total bust, I knew we were caught between flights. When asked, our young guide Chris confirmed the obvious. That we needed new birds.

That's why, when Jeff told us we had a goose hunt on tap for our last morning I was as dubious as the rest of the gang. Should have known better.

It was just short of an hour's drive to our field that morning, yet another barley field, this one freshly cut, with particularly highly fluffed swath. The type perfect to slip our blinds into. With the rig set Chris grabbed a handful of the fully headed crop and held it out for us to see. "There was well over a thousand darks on this crop yesterday afternoon. Our mission," he offered melodramatically, "should we accept it, is to shoot the birds off of it."

With grudging daylight that hazy morning came the sound of goose music ... lots of it ... filtering over the countryside from the none-too-distant roost. We warmed up on a couple of early flights of ducks. But after a single goose made the mistake of trying to stop in for breakfast, all went eerily silent. I was starting to think bad thoughts when the floodgates magically opened.

On they came then, barely topping the tree line to our east before setting sail for our rig. Flock after nice small flock finished as if they'd never seen a decoy before. Which, during this season anyway, they likely hadn't. The shooting was shamefully easy as we quickly pounded out limits in what was every bit, as far as we were concerned, THE classic of all classic Alberta goose shoots.

Turned out Jeff had been watching the show from the distance. When he drove into the field after it was over it was with the broadest grin imaginable on his much-relieved face. "Now, that's what I'm talkin' about!" he effused. "And so will we," I replied while extending my hand, "for a long time to come."

CHAPTER TWENTY-NINE

Truckin' with the T-Man

*M*aybe I'd just been lucky. In 30-plus years of Lab ownership ... or, more accurately ... having been owned by Labs ... I never had to deal with any serious doggy health issues. That is until one February evening in '05.

I was just kickin' back in the old recliner near the fireplace with Tanner lying at my feet. We were bathed in that good-tired feeling that comes after a long day of working and guiding at the game farm. All was right with our world.

When "T" stirred I watched as he uncharacteristically struggled to his feet. His haunches gave out first. His back end thumping the floor. Then, with his black nose pointed at the ceiling, his eyes rolled back in his head and he collapsed onto his side as his well-muscled body began to pound the hardwood in a violent, mouth-frothing seizure.

And so began his life as a Seizure Dog, as my vet called him. One that looked, early on, as if it would be a short one.

I was mortified at first. I mean, it couldn't be! Not my 6½-year-old all-star hunting, master-hunt-testing, often-sought-out stud dog. Not my buddy, the pup who'd come into my life at the same time I escaped the routine of having to go to the office every day, and who spent his time, pretty much at my side ever since.

Then, as the seizures became more frequent and more brutal I got scared, sensing we were headed down a dead-end road.

Finally, after thousands of dollars of diagnostics that proved negative, we embarked on a regimen of super-heavy drug dosages.

They stopped the seizures. And that was good. But they left the dog a droopy-eyed, stumbling, bumbling, dysfunctional, mere shadow of his former magnificent self. That was bad. And it wasn't right.

Being his only advocate I made the decision to trim the anti-convulsive meds, a combination of potassium bromide and phenobarbital, back to the point where Tanner regained function. If the seizures returned ... right or wrong ... I'd put him down. He just wasn't made to be a druggy. And he didn't deserve to take the beating of the inevitably severely damaging seizures.

We've been fortunate. It's been a good decision. Today we're out there doing what we've always done. But we're taking it one day at a time. Savoring each one as if it's our last. Our adventures since his "recovery" ... adventures that, scarily, might well have never happened ... have been nothing short of phenomenal.

The call came in April, barely a month after Tanner had recovered his coordination and most of his cognitive abilities. "Hey, Jack," the caller began in a familiar Canadian-tongued drawl. "It's Randy." "Yeah, I know. What's up bud?" I immediately asked in reply to my Manitoban friend, Randy Lewis.

"Well, me and the boys are getting set to give some of these late-spring snows a go. If you and Tanner can find your way up here," he challenged semi-sarcastically, "you're welcome to join in the fun."

And so we hopped in our ... er ... Tanner's truck and hit the familiar road, "T" on the back seat, and me, happily behind the wheel. As is his trademark, Randy had done his homework. The relatively few snows in the countryside nearby his Brandon home were widely scattered. But those he and his guiding buddies had located were happy, comfortable, and most importantly, huntable juveniles, many of which were left without adult supervision for the first time.

The hunting ... simply ... was as good as it gets. Five of us gunned something over 300 geese in four action-packed morning shoots. It was great to see Randy and the guys on the hunt, a busman's holiday for these hard-

working guides who spend the better time of each fall season putting their customers into the birds. But even better, was seeing Tanner perform.

Sharing the retrieving chores with another, younger, sometimes scrappy male yellow, he was a little more hyper than intense. And his handling wasn't as crisp as it could be, or had been. But he did all the long, hundred yard-plus marks, and all of the long blinds. And when he had the chance, he'd perform his patented, two-goose-at-a-time retrieves. All of this while sustaining several attacks from the ill-handled younger dog. Still, none of the work or the fights seemed to faze him. Other than he definitely was more tired after each outing than ever before.

I held my breath for days after the hunt, alert to the fact that it was after coming down from the "high" that he'd had seizures the fall before. But, knock on wood, they didn't happen.

We kept up our normal routine that following summer, training three to four times per week in a hunt test format, and conditioning every other day. We didn't run any tests because it was clear, thanks to the combination of damage from the seizures and the dulling effects of his drugs, that Tanner was no longer as sharp as the ever-more-picky judges would like to see. That said, he could still get the job done. He could still get the birds. And that's all that mattered to either of us.

Our super-busy fall began early, with a September trip to central Alberta. The only dog working for five guns, Tanner was pushed to the max, thanks to the fact that the shooting was world class. The duck shoots in particular, were stressful. Five-gun vollies, birds splashing into the grassy sloughs, tumbling into the stubble, and gliding, wounded, far over the hill ... often all at once ... produced a Herculean workload. One a ton larger than any a solitary dog should tackle. I'll admit it put me on edge. But there was no holding the guy back. If a seizure was ever work-related, Tanner was in for one. But, much to our relief, it never came.

Only days after returning home from our flying start to the season, we reloaded and headed out with our usual gang for a week in Manitoba with Randy. As always, the gunning was great. The result being dog work aplenty to be had. While the T-man got his share, so did the other dogs we hunted with each day. It was kind of strange though. Where as sharing the workload had never sat well with Tanner before, he seemed to accept it as a fact of life for the first time ever. And that was not a bad thing.

At the end of that fabulous week the boys packed up and headed back to Wisconsin. But we lingered behind. Tanner's Wonderful Adventure had a few weeks left to run.

Another good Canadian friend, Kevin McNeil, had invited us back to Alberta, first to be his guest for several days of hunting with clients, then to participate as a member of his crew in a Mossy Oak film shoot. We had a long haul in front of us, but Tanner and I were soon on the road again, this time westbound from Manitoba, tediously tooling through a Saskatchewan-wide snow storm, enroute to Peace Country.

I'll admit to getting a little homesick about this time. We were going to be out-of-country for quite a while, and a long haul from home. But I took solace from Tanner. He was a happy guy, and obviously could care less where we were as long as we were on the hunt, and he was with me. Thanks to regular phone conversations with Mary ... one mighty understanding lady ... I got over the gnawing, homesick feeling. So Tanner and

I proceeded to take advantage of the opportunity with an overriding, life-is-short attitude.

The first few days of hunting with Kevin and a couple of his clients from the east coast were nothing short of fantastic. With skies full of ducks and geese, many of which ended up over our gun barrels, all was well with our world. The only real test for Tanner came from Kevin's fiery, young, female black Lab. Totally unrestrained and breaking at every shot, watching her always get to the easy falls first, had him whining. But he survived, and in fact shined, as he marked his trademark, long-gliding woundies and handled all the blind retrieves.

While hunting for the camera is another story … another chapter … it's fair to say Tanner was stylin' during the film shoot. I'm not saying he was the better dog. Every man's dog … just because it's HIS dog … is afterall, the best dog. But Tanner was better trained than the other we hunted with, a young, black male, that like Kevin's, broke on every volley. Tanner's poise and experience were evident in that he got to do any and all of the more challenging retrieves.

Our return trip took us back through Russell, Manitoba where we got to make one last Canadian hunt for the season with Randy, Cyril, and Chubbs before returning stateside. And it proved to be the most special in a year of special hunts.

It had been a crisp, frosty, late October night, and setting up under a blanket of stars while the northern lights flashed across the night sky was a thankfully blood-warming task. With only a slightest suggestion of daylight in the east, on they came, early squadrons of hungry, chattering mallards targeting our barley field. "This is goin' to be a good one boys," Randy offered in an understated tone as we layed there with ducks landing all around us. "Drakes only. Let's make 'er last," he added.

When enough shooting light FINALLY arrived, we went to "work," but only casually. We were all enjoying the grand show … what might well be our last for the year … and no one wanted it to end. Only occasionally … when one of us could stand it no longer … would we take a greencap out.

It seemed that our dogs understood the gravity of the situation as well. Both Randy's Bullet, and Tanner, were uncharacteristically calm, almost stoic.

Even with all the often-technical work he had gotten, it seemed only fitting that Tanner's most memorable retrieve of that magical season came on this hunt. While returning with a plump, late-season greenhead at full gallop, yet another small, naïve flock of "northern" mallards lit right in his path. Without breaking stride he snapped up a second bird before it could flush ... another drake appropriately enough ... only to deposit both, quite matter-of-factly, into my waiting hand.

So our season-long hunt test-for-real had come to an end. And Tanner passed, seizure free!

But he's definitely not the dog he used to be. The formerly ever-intense, all-but-consumed-with-training-and-hunting hound has morphed into a classic, just-happy-to-be-a-dog dog. Proof I guess, that good can come from anything. No matter how dark it may seem at the time.

CHAPTER THIRTY

Huntin' for the Camera

*W*hen communicating the outdoor experience I always have been, and always will be, an old school fan of the written word. But all things change. Even though not always for the better.

We might not have to like it, but in our ever-more-fast-paced and technically oriented world the film media, through TV shows and DVDs, is having an ever-greater impact on outdoor communications. While we might not have to embrace it, we grudgingly have to accept it.

Though I admit to having had a natural curiosity about what's involved in hunting for the camera, I'd never sought to become involved in a film shoot. But then I'm undeniably the stubborn type. I have to "see for myself." So when Kevin McNeil asked that I join him in a hunt for Mossy Oak's camo cameras, and trusting his judgment when he stressed, "It'll be fun," I somewhat reluctantly agreed.

"Are you nuts?" one of my buddies, somewhat experienced with the TV thing, asked when I informed him of my decision. "You're goin' to regret it!," another stressed, adding, "It's a real pain in the butt!"

After questioning them further, it turned out both of these guys had been involved in film shoots that focused on a show's host/hero character. The type that would always have a camera trained just on him, and who'd babble a continuous, often meaningless commentary. What I was getting into with Kevin would be, or so he said, "Just a few of us regular types on a hunt. The only difference will be the cameras will be rolling, while we're having a good time."

Now I'm not sure, but it seemed Kevin was about to choke on his words half way through our first morning's goose hunt. After setting a beautiful decoy rig and fully stubbling our blinds ... doing all we could do really ... the birds we'd scouted feeding in our field for three days straight were doing nothing but flipping us off. We weren't shooting birds. And that was bad enough. But our cameramen, situated one each in the rather obtrusive bale and willow stick blinds, were noticeably silent. They weren't getting the footage they'd come for. And Kevin was feeling the pressure. Topping it off was the fact that we'd all but run out of good-natured banter. There wasn't much to say. Only geese over the decoys could spice things up. It was reality TV at its finest, or worst, depending on your perspective.

Then finally, with the birds beginning to trickle back to the roost, the action started to pick up. It wasn't spectacular. But we fooled enough flocks of one to three birds to pull off a dandy little backshoot that produced 18 geese. Though far short of our potential 56-bird limit, we had enough, we were told, for a show.

Kevin had a duck hunt planned for the afternoon as our three-truck caravan rolled across a field of barley stubble toward a distant tree line. I wished Kevin had thought to give me some warning for my still camera. But the boys with the camo cameras were about beside themselves when we topped the field's last rise only to witness the grandest of scenes ... one Kevin fully anticipated but failed to mention ... as thousands of mallards, each producing its own mini-geyser, began to explode off the beaver pond. It was a sight we could have/should have recorded on film.

We hustled to take up positions in the scrub along the pond's edge, confident ... even cocky ... to a man, that this hunt would be a no-brainer. And it would have been had we gotten right down to business. But oh no, being the rock stars we were, we took our time, tossing a few decoys, all the while hamming it up for the camera. When finally finished, Kevin instructed authoritatively, "OK boys. We'll take 'em one man, one greenhead at a time. I'll call the shot."

By then half the ducks we'd jumped had tried to return, but all we did was haze them off. Big mistake. The ducks relocated, and our big time

shoot never materialized later on. In the end, once again, we managed just enough birds to get some footage. But Kevin was far from happy, realizing what could have been.

Knowing we hadn't really messed with these ducks to a major extent, Kevin planned a field shoot ... in a pea field at that ... on them the following morning.

With a healthy breeze beginning to kick out of the west, we worked under cover of darkness to set a rig that would allow us to crosswind the birds. Something we needed to do for the sun-shy cameras. Even as we settled in to await needed camera light, we were overrun by flight after ground-scraping flight of mallards, many of which would land and begin feeding, happily chattering away as they marched, like so many toy soldiers, right among our blinds.

"Oh, this is going to be sweet!" one of our guys allowed as the rest of us pretty much babbled on incoherently, not unlike the bunch of overaged little kids we really were.

It was a tough wait to say the least, as quite literally thousands of naïve, never-been-hunted, oh-so-hungry mallards worked us. We were enduring a sensory overload, the sights and sounds, due to their sheer volume, quite unlike anything I'd ever experienced in my duck world.

When Rusty, one of the cameramen finally announced, "OK guys. Have at 'em!" we were actually a tad reluctant to do so. As Kevin, our leadman, rambled on about the "awesome" experience he made us pass, time and again, on the building flocks backpedaling in our face. Only when Rusty barked, "Come on now. My battery's gettin' low!" did Kevin make the call.

Tanner, wound tight and trembling, with paws dug deep into the fine prairie soil like a sprinter in the starting blocks, predictably broke at the volley as greenheads rolled in the bright blue sky, only to smack the earth in a pleasant series of dust-raising thuds. For a moment chaos reigned. I caught myself before I could cuss "T" out, realizing only at the last instant that salty language ... a normal part of any situation involving shotguns and high-powered canines ... was a no-no when the microphones were on.

Even though enveloped in a world of quacking fowl we continued, quite unintentionally, to challenge our poor cameramen. Time and again we'd have the heart of the decoying flock hanging in our faces at my end of the line of shooters, and right smack in the middle of Rusty's camera window where he wanted/needed to record the kill shots to authenticate the hunt. But Kevin lost track of the fact that film footage was really job one, as he fell, quite naturally, into the guide's role of getting shooting for all of his hunters. Had this been a film-free hunt we'd have taken the time to simply reposition our hunters so everyone could take advantage of how the birds were working the wind. But relocating the camera gear to accommodate such a move, from a time constraint perspective alone, would have been impractical. Not to mention that it was impossible, given the position of the sun. So it goes, we learned, with the challenges involved in hunting for the camera.

Given that solitary glitch, and thanks to the sheer numbers of ducks, this hunt, much to Kevin's relief, played out just as he'd hoped. By its end everyone, myself included, was happy and totally at ease. It had, as Kevin promised, been a ton of FUN.

So, would I want to hunt for the cameras on a routine basis? Hell no! It's just not natural for me to not be able to cuss out loud about my often shoddy shooting. And not being able to use the "____ damnit" command ... the one he respects the most ... with Tanner, is like cutting my dog-handling right hand off.

CHAPTER THIRTY-ONE

Gone to the Dogs

*T*hough we don't dwell on it, given today's societal pressures, there remains the nagging question. Why? Why do we hunt?

A lot sharper, a lot more literary minds than mine have pondered and addressed that question. Maybe to our satisfaction. Maybe not.

But I'm here to tell you, once you've witnessed the pure unadulterated drive ... the sheer love of doing what it was born to do ... that a well-bred canine exhibits in pursuit of game, you'll never question, or let yourself ever be questioned again, as to why you do it. You'll only wish you could hunt with so much who-gives-a-damnwhat-anyone thinks, natural, instinctive inhibition.

If you don't find yourself, both in envy and awe of the gun dog, then when it comes to bird hunting, FORGET IT!

My introduction to the wonderful world of dogs came one wintry Saturday afternoon almost a lifetime ago. I'm not exactly sure, but I was no more than 8 or 9 years old, when my mother stuffed the $.35 price of admission into my hand and sent me, along with a neighborhood friend, off to the Sheboygan Theater for the afternoon matinee. It was a steep price to pay, (the usual weekend afternoon price per child was 25 cents), but Disney movies commanded a premium.

I don't recall a lot of the details, other than the film's melancholy, sad-to-glad ending. One that brought tears to my eyes. (And I wasn't alone. There wasn't a dry eye in the house.) But I was mesmerized, then as now, by the portrayal of the wonderful and unique relationship ... the bond ... that exists between boy/man and dog.

I knew that day, after experiencing Old Yeller, that there was a yellow dog in this boy's future. Little did I realize then, that it would be nearly 20 years before I became owned by my first four-legged hunting partner.

Shamus

At the time Mary, I, and our two boys were living in North Hudson. A career move had taken us to the St. Croix River Valley and the nearby Twin Cities, from where I traveled as my job demanded. For the first time we had a home and a yard with immediate access to enough open country to work and run a dog. So, with no more excuses and Mary's blessing, I went shopping for the first yellow dog, that if nothing else, would be a color match for our tow-headed youngsters.

Big-headed and a jumble of uncoordinated legs at 14 weeks of age, the happy-go-lucky pup was the last of a litter of well-bred ... we were told but really didn't care ... chocolates and yellows. The brown pups, the yuppie's color of choice, went first, then the yellow females, leaving this rambunctious, red-colored male on his own.

Starved for attention, the gangly pup was friendly enough. "But does he have what it takes? Can this dog hunt?" I naively asked. In response the trainer/kennel owner grabbed a pigeon, plucked its flight feathers, and tossed it, repeatedly, for the thrilled-to-get-a-chance-to-fetch youngster. Each time, though naturally a bit chewy, the little red dog retrieved it, first to the trainer's, then, when I offered it, my hand.

As far as my inexperienced eyes could see, the pooch was already doing everything I needed it to. "Sold," I said. And Shamus was on his way home with us. Why we didn't wreck enroute I'll never know, because I spent as much time watching the grinning puppy in the wagon's rear view mirror as I did the road.

So began 12 years of canine adventure. It's fair to say I trained the dog, in those e-collarless days, only instinctively. I hand-threw him bumpers on a daily basis, and took him hunting as often as I could. If it had feathers, we chased it. Grouse, woodcock, pheasants, ducks, or geese, it didn't matter, "Famous Shamus," (by then I'd begun scribbling and had published a few of our adventures along with pix of the yellow dog on-the-job), was up to the challenge. But above all, snow geese were our game, and on the North Dakota prairie was where we played it.

There never was a more free spirit than Shamus as he shot across the wheat stubble in a cloud of dust, often cresting a rise, streaking out of sight, only to return, still at full gallop, but minutes later with that long-gliding woundie locked firmly in his maw. An otherwise likely lost bird he could then add to the pile he so proudly guarded.

At 98 pounds of solid muscle, Shamus was a force to be reckoned with as a ton of birds found out. And so did the timid meter man, or anyone else that strangely approached our home, vehicle, Mary, or the boys.

But he was hard-headed, and at times disobedient to a fault. Almost all of his life, when he didn't want to hear it, he simply didn't listen. And in his last years he was so deaf from being around gunfire, he couldn't. At least that's my excuse, and I'm stickin' to it.

Sadie

Sadie came into our lives less than two years before her father, Shamus, passed. A perfect example of what selective breeding can do, Saderue was

a 50/50 blend of her parents. She had all the size and drive of Shamer, but the light-to-white color and more tractable nature of her mother, Ginger, buddy Dave Warnke's female.

Even though born to take his place ... and I'm sure Shamus sensed just that ... he accepted her into his, as quickly as she wound herself into our lives. Pretty intolerant of any other canines attempting to do his work, it was strange how gracefully he handled alternating retrieving chores with Sadie on her first, and his last NoDak trip.

As she grew and learned we found there was nothing Shamus could do that Sadie couldn't do, and often a little better. And thanks to her introduction to the electronic collar half way through her life, she made me appear at least a 100% better trainer, (which isn't saying much), than I had been with Shamus.

Like her father, Sadie had a full life, the highlight of which had to be her sixth year. She performed at a championship level during nine days of the best snow goose hunting we'd ever experienced to that point. Then, during back to back SoDak and Iowa pheasant trips, proved our go to dog and top producer. At her athletic prime, she even ran down and caught a jackrabbit in full flight. Though the unfortunate bunny helped the cause, zigging when it should have zagged.

Her life as a gun dog aside, she was a wonderful family pet as well. Her sole fault being that should she get the chance, she'd lick a burglar to death. There wasn't a mean or defiant bone in her powerful, boyishly built body. A happy dog if there ever was once, I'll never forget her tail-wagging approach to water retrieves. Only after she got her mouth on the bird or bumper did she allow her tail to settle in and serve its purpose as a rudder.

It was Sadie's good fortune too, to come along later in my life. Since my career allowed just a little more time, she got that much more of it. As a result she enjoyed doing even more of her thing ... hunting ... than did her father.

Tanner

Tanner came along before I was ready for him. I was in denial I suppose, not wanting to face the facts with Sadie Lady. But Mary, bless her, knew it was time. Upon my return from a northern Wisconsin deer hunt Mary announced, "I found a dandy yellow puppy. Let's go take a look at him." Only reluctantly did I agree.

Now, I'm not a real puppy guy I guess. Only after seeing what a dog can really do ... seeing it work ... am I impressed. So, it wasn't love at first sight.

I mean, I liked the little guy well enough. But he was just that. Another little pup, not much unlike the rest of the black and yellow litter.

We left the breeder's without making a commitment. But on the drive home Mary asked what I thought. "Well, I don't know ... " I started. Then Mary interrupted, stating firmly, "You can take him now, or you'll find him under the Christmas tree."

So we spun around, (I know when the boss has spoken), and picked the yellow fluff ball up. Looking at him nestled contentedly on Mary's lap as we once again turned for home it came to me. "Tanner. We'll name him Tanner because he's tanner than Sadie," I not so brilliantly concluded.

"T" came on board. And his timing was impeccable. I was ready to pull the pin on a career and that would give me the chance to spend all the time I wanted with my pooch, for the first time in my life.

Fortunately, for both Tanner and me, I became acquainted, and fast friends with Mike Lambrecht and his wife, Dariel, as the precocious pup turned 6 months of age, and just before my ineptitude could ruin him. Mike and Dariel are avid Chessie breeders, and Mike is a gonzo retriever trainer. Thanks to his tutelage, Tanner and I got off on the right "feet."

With the basics having been pounded in place, and Tanner's championship lineage, we embarked on an intermittent, but successful hunt test campaign, and a major hunting career, that to this point has given Tanner, quite literally, thousands of birds. Now, at age 8, having been up and down the flyway with me each autumn and spring, and having served as the top dog on the game farm I ran for six years, he is no doubt my best trained, most talented, (if not my favorite, because each of a man's dogs is that in its time), gundog ever. That said, it's only his vast experience, having hunted from dog-boxed pit blind, treestands in flooded timber, all manner of watercraft, and countless field hunt setups, that make him so.

While Tanner has led somewhat of a charmed existence, it's not been without some major bumps in the road. He's become afflicted with seizures. Though controlled by meds, they've left him today not all that he once was. (But then so does the aging process, I'm finding, put each of

Tanner

us in the same predicament.) Still, as I look at him while I write this, I'm hopeful he'll have a lot more of those special moments. And I know that if I give him the chance ... and you can bet I will ... he'll be performing his patented two-snow-geese-at-a-time retrieves for years to come.

(Yeah, I know two birds at once is not cool by doggy game standards. But in hunting it's practical. Especially for a dog as greedy as the T-man, who only wants each and every bird all for himself.)

Maggie

Maggie, sweet Maggie … now there's a rescue story if there ever was one.

There came the time that our son, Billy, was looking for his first Lab. Preferably a female, so Tanner would be sure to get along with it, and housebroken, so his landlord would allow it.

Mary found the ad in the local paper. It read "Two year old yellow female, spayed, all shots." When we called on it we were thrilled to find Maggie had the same parents as Tanner, from a repeat breeding two years later than his.

I was at Maggie's door the next morning where the Mrs. struggled to control one, obviously high-powered, playful, white-colored Lab. When I asked if I could take her for an evaluation, the young lady all but pushed the eager dog at me. As she loaded willingly into the kennel box in the back of my truck I noticed her unusually soft pads. "Carpet paws," Mary would call them. She'd obviously been maintained as the trophy suburban pet she was or wasn't destined to be. We'd see.

I hauled Maggie over to Mike's to get his reading on her prospects. In a short half hour we went from firing a remote starter pistol and tossing a wing-clipped pigeon, to shooting a full-grown mallard over her, which she happily handled, retrieving it to hand like a seasoned pro. Considering she'd never been near gunfire or birds before, it was quite the lesson in the importance of good breeding.

Greeting me with a hopeful look and a handful of leashes, Maggie's soon-to-be-past-owner couldn't take my $200 (what a steal!) fast enough. We were outa' there. And Maggie never looked back.

The next day Maggie met Billy, and the two of them proceeded to find, shoot, and retrieve six chuckars and a pair of roosters at our Happy Dog game farm. With all but no formal training, the made-for-each-other pair has been bringing home the bacon ever since. No matter what upland or waterfowling scenario Billy puts Maggie in, she excels naturally. Hunting right next to them, Maggie doesn't know or care that she isn't a "big" dog in a well-trained sense.

Whether traveling and living in Billy's pickup, at home on the couch with me, or in the field, Maggie sweet Maggie, is living the life she was meant to.

Through the years I've been exposed to, and have had the pleas-ure of hunting with a ton of canine talent. Way too much to re-count. But there are a remarkable few who are worthy of note.

The Black Dog of Minnedosa

It was the first morning of the first ever Canadian hunt back in the early '70s. Bob Kovacic, buddy Dave's dad, and I teamed up to hunt a small sheet water pond we found plastered with a mixture of gadwal, wigeon, and mallards. After flushing the birds we simply slithered into the swath plan-ning to greet the returnees with loads of #5s.

It didn't take long to burn our little honey hole, and while picking up our half dozen birds, I noticed ducks pouring into a quarter mile-distant slough. Bob wanted to hang tight, but I decided to make the little move. Exploding at my approach, the brown ducks began to circle back even as I took cover in the hole's cattail fringe. No sooner than I did, a small, mixed-flock of gadwall and wigeon attacked my position. I rose to greet them, dropping a pair of gads with my three-shot salute. One bird tumbled into the tulies on my side of the pond. The other crashed 35 yards off, across the open water.

Easy marks I thought, but not for long. Try as I might, I couldn't find ei-ther duck in the thickly woven, heavily matted cover. I was damn disgusted when I looked up to see the big black dog standing in profile atop the nearby rise. "What the hell?!" I thought. So I not-so-cleverly hollered, "Here boy!"

Short of leg and thick of body, it was easy to see this happy-looking, bright-eyed Lab was a nice guy. I hadn't a clue about how to handle him so I simply took him downwind of where I figured the first fall to be and told him ... again, none-too-intelligently ... to "Hunt it up." Which he did, in a matter of seconds. Repeating the process, he found my second bird al-most as quickly.

I was a happy camper. Thanking the big boy by rubbing his ears I took off to meet back up with Bob. "Who's your friend?" Bob queried upon my return. Only then did I turn to see "my" black dog standing 10 paces behind me, happily wagging his tail and with a wrinkled brow, hopeful look in his yellow eyes.

Try as we might, we couldn't shake the guy. Once back at the wagon he stood there, looking like he wanted to jump in. Which is exactly what he did ... just like he did it every day ... upon our offer. With no tags or collar, we figured, in the worst case, to take him to town with us and ask around as to who his owner might be.

The black dog hunted with us the rest of that day, teaching us firsthand, just how valuable a bird-smart gun dog can be. Even when a couple of our guys crept a pothole, black dog belly crawled right along with them, just as he must have done a hundred times before.

As our day's hunt came to an end we debated what to do with our newfound companion. Should we bring him to town and ask around? Or should we turn him out where we found him? Thinking and hoping he'd know his way home.

We opted for the latter. Feeling better about our decision as black dog decisively trotted up the hill on which I first found him, stopping at its crest to give us a short, seemingly farewell glance.

Having related our experience to the manager of our hotel, we were much-relieved to find we'd made the right call. "Oh, that's farmer so-and-so's Lab. If he hears any gunfire, that huntin' fool'll go lookin' for it, eh? He's more that happy to hunt for anyone who'll let 'im. Not to worry. You can bet he's home, warm, well-fed ... and thanks to you guys ... quite happy tonight."

The black dog of Minnedosa reminded me of all I ever wanted my hunting dog ... whenever I finally got one ... to be.

Rocky

It was a cold, drizzly, downright ugly late March morning in eastern SoDak. Buddy and spring snow goose fanatic John DeVries had us set up in a muddy, still snow-banked field of corn stubble.

We heard them long before they materialized out of the ooze, three snows, ghost-like apparitions in our dark, gray world. Hanging over my side of the spread I cut loose, rocking the leader twice, then whiffing with my desperate third shot. The tough old bird powered on, finally buckling a good 400 yards out over a field of winter wheat.

I looked at John, his gaze transfixed on Rocky, his big, black, classically block-headed Lab.

"Naw!" I offered.

"Oh yeah," John replied, "he's got 'em!"

John growled "RRRRockay!" and the pooch was off on a line that took him through a flooded sheet water pond, over a snow-drifted fenceline, and then directly on to the goose.

It was experienced dog work at its finest.

Rocky came to John at 1½ years of age as a washed out field trial prospect. His work was excellent, and on a par with that of a sibling who went on to become a renowned field champion. But his hips were bad.

And so began Rocky's storied hunting career. Rocky was a lover, and a bit of a clown. And he could as quickly worm his way into any dog man's heart, as he could his lunch box. But most of all, that dog could hunt. By the time he was seven, Rocky had logged in excess of 10,000 hunting retrieves. But by age 8, those hips caught up with him. Aside from an occasional solo hunt with John, he was, of necessity, prematurely retired.

Rocky lived the life a gun dog was meant to. For my money, he was one for the ages.

Haus

When I first met Haus he took me by surprise. Stepping around the back of Mike Lambrecht's Explorer I came face to face with one very impressive Chessy. With those wolf-like yellow eyes boring a hole through me, and a huge head pressed up against the kennel box door that struck me as no match for him, I took a step back. But there was no violent reaction. He just sat there, calm as could be.

Haus, misspelled, but named after Hoss Cartwright, certainly fit the character's bill. Sturdily built, with a massive, imposing head, he had the heart of the western's gentle giant. And the talent of its actor.

Haus was a Master class hunt test dog and the standard against which we trained when my Tanner was a pup. There wasn't a conceivable set of marks that Haus couldn't handle. And his blinds were truly a thing of beauty. A spirited animal, he always worked with unbridled enthusiasm, and that's what would get him into trouble. The guy was rock solid 95% of the time, but would break when least expected.

Though he ran some beautiful tests, it was his first real hunt that I remember most.

Mike and Haus joined us one fall on their first ever Canadian prairie hunt. We got into a heck-of-a-good shoot that first morning, one we'd set aside strictly for Haus. Kind of dumfounded at first, with four or five "marks" falling from the sky with each nine- or 10- shot volley, Haus finally got with the program, happily making 39 retrieves. Amazingly, Mike was so into his dog's work that he never fired a shot! Though arguable, it may have been their best day ever.

Haus was robbed of a full career, prematurely succumbing to cancer at age 8. I'm sure I speak for Mike when I say to Haus, "Thanks for the memories."

CHAPTER THIRTY-TWO

Ducks for Bucks... The Dollars and Sense of Waterfowling's Future

Anyone who has found the world of wildfowl to be so meaningful in their lives is bound to reach a point where we ponder, and become concerned about its future. In this respect, I'm no different.

As I've done so ... all the good and wondrous times I've been fortunate enough to experience not withstanding ... I initially found it difficult to not become a little depressed and pessimistic. Given the socio-economic pressures that drive our ever-more-complicated world today, it can be next-to-impossible to comprehend just how waterfowling will fit ... hell, even exist ... in our world as it speeds so quickly forward.

My lack of foresight early on, I came to realize, was attributable in great part to being caught in the same box I see the majority of waterfowlers stuck in today.

Today's enthusiast is more than happy to attend a D.U., Delta, or any similar state-based organization's fund raising dinner. There he happily drops his $200 and walks away feeling good about himself. Feeling he's done his part.

Well, while what he's done isn't bad ... and will help the cause ... it's far, sadly, from the answer. And this is why.

Just take a look at the Conservation Reserve Program (CRP) as it exists in the Farm Bill today. Nothing in the history of North America ... not all the National Wildlife Refuges, not all of the wetland or grassland easements purchased or leased, not all the efforts of our leading conservation organizations combined, throughout their entire histories ... has produced the wildfowl, (not to mention pheasants, deer, songbirds, and other wildlife), that, with one stroke of the legislative pen, has the habitat created by CRP!

Only water, that uncontrollable cyclic phenomena, can do more for ducks.

As for purchasing enough land, outright or through easements, forget it! What landowners do is own land. They'll never sell, and we'll never be able to afford to buy enough habitat to maintain, much less grow, our wildfowl populations.

What we as concerned sportsmen fail to realize, but what our biologists are keenly aware of, and most landowners, but regrettably few legislators already know, is that it's only effective land use legislation that will adequately support and grow our wildfowl populations. Finally realizing this,

What We Can Do ...

The old refrain is "write your representatives." And that is what we should do. But we rarely get around to it.

Instead, support the conservation group(s) of your choice. Ideally those, or at least the one that does the best job of lobbying.

If I had to pick just one organization it would be Pheasants Forever. Their work on the Farm Bill ... specifically on The Conservation Reserve Program (CRP) ... since the '80s is a model when it comes to producing effective land use legislation.

I've become nothing if not optimistic about the future of the resource and our sport. I'll tell you why.

Because it makes economic sense!

It's the economy, after all, that makes our world go round. And farming marginal land ... land that only in rare years produces a viable crop ... is bad for the economy. Subsidizing a landowner to farm marginal land, to spend the labor, fuel, fertilizer, herbicide, pesticide, and seed inputs, to produce nothing, (as is commonly the case with the current Farm Bill), is not only unproductive, it's counter-productive! It's a drag on an economy that relies on productivity gains to grow.

Landowners who enroll in CRP do so because they're money ahead idling marginally productive land.

Whether it's CRP or some other similar land use legislation, I have to believe it will continue to be part of the Farm Bill, only because it's in the best interest of our country's, even the world's, ECONOMY.

It's a simple formula really.

Landowner Payment greater (>) than the Value of Crop minus (-) the cost of all labor, fuel, and other inputs required to produce it.

Just look at the energy we'd save and the emissions we'd prevent alone!

What all of this simple, economic theory boils down to is, that if we compensate the landowner fairly, as he should be, he'll happily set aside his marginal land and develop the habitat that will produce our birds. While the rallying cry at so many banquets is, "Let's spend some bucks for the ducks," let's start thinking outside that box. Realize that it's the legislatively incented private landowner ... the landowner who's already re-

On Ethanol ...

The latest pressure being brought to bare on our ever-valuable-for-wildlife, marginal farmlands is that of raising corn for ethanol production.

Whether it's corn or any other annual crop, marginal land is marginal land. It only rarely produces a viable crop. In the meantime the cost of inputs is a waste and a drag on the economy. A situation that is magnified if we tolerate legislation that subsidizes the attempted cropping.

Allowing the periodic harvest of native grasses on marginal land, in lieu of that year's CRP payment, (as Pheasants Forever is proposing), to produce cellulosic ethanol MAY be a viable option.

sponsible for producing more than 90% of our ducks ... who'll produce even more Ducks for Bucks.

Let's by all means continue to support our fine conservation organizations. They're doing many, many great things. But let's encourage them to join together, with the outdoor industry, (the gun, boat, ammo, camo, and gear manufacturers, the retailers, and outfitter organizations), to present a united front ... one that represents huge economic force in total ... to lobby for that all-important, effective land use legislation. Form a Political Action Committee (a PAC) to work for us in Washington. Like it or not, that IS how things get done in the country.

Rather than strictly servicing our individual agendas, we need to work together. It only makes Dollars and Sense, for the economy, AND the ducks.

CHAPTER THIRTY-THREE

The Guides

In 45 years of banging around the world of wildfowling it was inevitable that I'd have my share of experiences with guides. Maybe I've been lucky. But with a few notable exceptions, they've been positive and additive to the hunt. Still, those that weren't are nearly as memorable.

My worst guided experience, bar none, was with a self-professed, "full-time professional waterfowl guide" working over the spring snow goose flights passing through Squaw Creek in northwest Missouri. Hunting with this guy was just that: hunting with him while paying to support his gunning habit. He'd regularly call and fire the first shot, invariably taking the "candy" bird for himself. Then he'd openly berate us, his clients, for whiffing on the wildly flaring, by then way too tall birds. Quickly coming to understand his game, I, much to his dismay, began to call my own shots, taking time only to explain that it was my hunt I was paying for, and I'd conduct it as I damn well pleased. If not a good one, hunting with this guy was a learning experience.

Another time I was on a hunt in the Cajun country of southwestern Louisiana's Cameran Parish. Our young outfitter really had a fine little operation going, with decent lodging, great meals, and prime flooded rice fields to hunt. But once on the hunt, he proved far too serious. Killing birds, as many as possible, was paramount to him, as he felt it should be to his customers.

Part of my motivation on that trip was to have my then young Lab gain some valuable and varied experience. But, not having been beat into total, stay down-steady, flinchless submission like his own dog, it was easy to see that Tanner's less than impeccable manners nearly drove our guide's obvi-

ously hot temper past the boiling point. Gritting his teeth and staying tight-lipped as he knew he should, he handed us off to his more easy going guiding partner for the rest of our stay. Still, the tension this paying customer's dog created, but shouldn't have from our host's perspective, took the edge off the whole experience.

Then there was our young guide on a Saskatchewan adventure. Amiable enough, the youngster, working for his distant outfitter boss, would set us up each morning, then leave us to the hunt. And that was fine. But his priorities weren't with us. Gunning coyotes over his prized carcass pile, (instead of scouting), and getting us out of the field in time for his grandmother to sell us breakfast at midmorning, (even if the birds were still flying), seemed uppermost on his mind. But overall, the hunt went fine. And the "no charge" evening bull sessions helping his story-telling grandfather imbibe in the fruits of the home still, were a bonus.

"Jeffy" was the guide and the experience in and of himself. Young, skinny, but wiry, the kid was a legend in his own mind, no doubt due in great part to the fact that his brother owned the operation. The young Canuck made quite the first impression. Literally bursting into our room on the eve preceding our first hunt, he laid down the law ... or at least thought he did ... not unlike a drill sergeant. "I'll call the shots, and no dogs allowed," were two of the most inflammatory statements he could make to me. "We'll see about that buddy. Let's get something straight right from the start. This is our hunt, not yours!" I, with the authority of seniority, countered. Slamming the door behind him, our battle of wills had begun.

The pre-dawn, nearly hour-long high speed, dash over and along a winding series of Manitoban backroads was ridiculous. But the old man (me) kept his foot in it as I chased Jeff's dust trail. BS'ing him as we finally ground to a stop, I allowed that the run was the most fun I'd had since "I" was a "kid."

From the get go it was obvious that "Mr. Personality" knew his birds ... well ... at least where to find them. He learned in short order that we, (including our dogs, much to his dismay), were no slouches when it came to hunting them. If our relationship wasn't warm and fuzzy, it was founded on mutual respect. And so, after a needlessly rocky start, we got through the week just fine.

With guides, I'd come to learn that you never really know what to expect. And no one proved that point more than our mostly native Canadian friend on a trip to Manitoba's big lake country.

After a long, twisting, turning, disorienting boat ride out into a sprawling Lake Winnepegosis, our man gunned the engine, sending us sliding into the tulies at "the spot." All was quiet at first, but as the sun torched a crack between the water's chopping eastern horizon and the lifting overcast, the birds began to move. Lines of divers scraped the wave tops, and rushing flocks of puddlers materialized overhead from the still dark western sky.

While we waited for shooting light our guide casually queried, "Do you mind?" lighting up before we could reply. I made little of it at first, but then I noticed the "weed" wasn't a tobacco cigarette at all. What could we say? It was too late to stop him, and I doubt we could have anyway.

So there we were, in an unfamiliar, wilderness setting, in the hands of a daylight toker. The man knew his birds though, and how they "played the game," as he'd dreamily put it, at each spot he took us to.

Still, it was an uncomfortable, even potentially dangerous situation as one mishap proved. I was in the bow watching our guy twist the throttle on the 30-horse outboard as we went to relocate. As if in slow motion the ill-fastened engine, by its own torque, twisted right off the transom. The look of sheer terror on our there-to-fore impaired guide's suddenly sober face, as the motor went down running, was one I'll never forget. But its one I never need to see again.

We survived. But just as easily couldn't have.

I first met John DeVries one snowy, bitter, early March day in eastern Nebraska. He left no doubt, right from the outset, that he was an addict if there ever was one. And waterfowl, snow geese in particular, were his drug of choice.

Within minutes of our initial handshake, John morphed into his alter ego, the great white goose. Then he set about "flying" about the motel room on bowed wings (arms) explaining to anyone who'd listen (me) ... who I'll admit was mired somewhere in the middle ground between dumfounded and awestruck ... how geese communicate. How they actually talk ... in articulate conversations ... to one another, as he, to this day, believes they do. Hardly an act, it's a routine that I've seen John spring into time and again over the years. And it's one I never tire of, for its always subtly different twists and turns. Never knowing what he'll come up with next, John keeps me on the edge of my seat.

I initially started hunting with John as his client and as such, took my share

of guff from him. Too many long days and short nights of guiding, I learned, could make John a dull, even ill-tempered boy. But nothing ... come rain, snow, hell, or high water ... can dim his pure enthusiasm for the hunt. And there's a lesson in that.

Argentinian Alec Byrne was a study in square-jawed toughness. A former professional rugby player with the blown out knee to show for it, the shaggy-haired, black-bearded, and dark-eyed one proved the consummate professional as he guided Brian French and I through the windblown hinterlands of southern Patagonia in search of the Magellan goose.

Thanks to Alec's substantial efforts, more than just a hunt, ours was more a pure adventure. One of only two English-speaking people we met during our five-day stay in this harsh land along the straights of Magellan, he expertly handled the logistics, prepared midday feasts afield that featured not only great meats and breads, but tablecloths and wines in the finest of European traditions. But most importantly, he put us into the birds.

Bad leg and all, Alec, along with his sidekick Fabrizio, would strike out at first light to walk-up, or haze the otherwise contentedly grazing geese toward our decoy spread. After a typical shoot we'd have the ground fairly littered with birds, which Alec and Fabrizio would strap up and hump back to the truck. Watching Alec muck through the lowlands in ill-fitting hippers, toting strings of 15 or so 9-pound geese, all the time with a trademark grin on his face, was a sight to see.

So too was the last glimpse I had of him as we boarded our plane in Rio Gallegos for the return trip.

Alec had rented a brand new Ford pickup for our hunt. I don't know what the issue was, the dent in the rear quarter panel he'd put in it as he side-slipped into the bank during a river crossing, or the fact that he may have returned it to the airport livery a day or two late. But the two wide-bodied enforcer-types that had Alec sandwiched as they led him off to conduct their "business," seemed more than a little agitated.

It's probably just a coincidence, but we never heard from Alec again.

My Hudson Bay experience was notable, not only for the unique hunting this mystical land of the muskeg offered, but for the unexpected cultural experience it provided. Reading of it in *Outdoor Life* as a youngster, I longed for the day when I could venture to Hudson's Bay and hunt geese mouth-called by the Cree. When that day finally came, I got far move than bargained for, thanks to Louis Bird, our 65-year-old-guide.

Oh, Louie, a jolly and gentle sort, could talk to the geese alright, bringing flock after family sized staging flock into shotgun range. But between flights he had a lot more to say. He spoke of the fact that his people are not, as commonly communicated, Cree at all. His tribe, the native inhabitants of the southwest coast of

Hudson Bay and the west coast of James Bay, are more accurately known as the Omushkigowack (people of the muskeg). He bemoaned the fact that he and the other guides were old men, and that none of the younger generation, content to live in town on the white man's subsidies, were interested in carrying on the traditions. In Louis' vocation of storyteller for the tribe, he explained he'd made it his life's ambition to record and publish, the entire "legend" (history) of his people.

I don't know if Louis accomplished his goal, but as much as he shared with us in our brief time together, it was good to know we taught him something as well. Louie absolutely delighted to Steve Loebaka's delicatedly seasoned, pan-fried pintail breasts, finding them far more palate-friendly than his people's traditional practice of simply boiling their fowl.

Hunting with Rick Reynolds in coastal southwestern Alaska was a study in competition. Bushy blond-haired, bearded, and always hatless inspite of the ever-present precipitation, Rick appears every bit the rough and tumble Viking. A pilot of ships and bush planes, a commercial fisherman, a deckland on the deadly crab boats, and a waterfowl guide, Rick is your classic, do-whatever-it-takes, season-to-season, Alaskan. Maybe it's his instinctive need to hustle the next opportunity ... the next buck ... that makes Rick so competitive. But it's a fact not lost on his hunters.

Gunning right along with us, it was soon apparent that Rick wanted to be ... hell, fully intended to be ... top gun. And he was willing to make a wager to that effect, betting on his ability to out-slog us through the tidal flats. Realizing that pass-shooting was what he was all about, we took that bet.

Young and strong each, my son Billy, along with Levi Hendrickson from Minnesota, took Rick on heads up. And they more than held their own, coming back with straps that, much to his dismay, matched or bettered Rick's. But both lads admitted they paid the price in terms of effort expended.

Steve Loebaka and I chose to deploy a small rig of decoys barely a block inland from the beach. Though laying out in the salt-slimy mud and sparsely grassed cover wasn't the most pleasant experience, quickly taking our birds as they classically worked to us, more than made up for it. We easily waxed Rick, and with a lot less physical effort. Something of which I sensed Rick made note. I'm not certain, but I'd bet Rick is regularly gunning over decoys these days.

―――――――――――――――――――――

Of all the guide/outfitters I've dealt with through the years, none have been so professional and accommodating as Randy Lewis of Brandon, Manitoba. Barely 30 years of age when I first met him, Randy, a police officer by profession, is mature beyond his years.

Living in God's country when it comes to waterfowling, Randy works diligently to put his hunters in the best of the best situations, and has provided many a hunt-of-a-lifetime for his clients, including myself. His appreciation of the birds is apparent, but it's his love of the hunt that really motivates him. He takes great pride and satisfaction in finding and producing quality hunts, something he does with amazing regularity.

To hunt with Randy and his guys is to build a lasting relationship. No doubt most of his customers, like myself, are happy to call Randy, friend.

―――――――――――――――――――――

There are a lot of good and interesting characters out there in the wide world of waterfowl guides, and each, I've found, puts his own signature on the hunt. Sean Mann, the renowned call maker takes center stage, entertaining his customers with an almost musical, but virtuoso calling performance that is second-to-none. Kevin McNeil of Blue Sky Outfitters up in Alberta's Peace River country, who is anything but a showboat, is only concerned with making his customers happy. "If they're happy, I'm happy," he simply and sincerely states. Todd Jackson, owner of Penobscot Bay Outfitters in Maine is nothing if not intense. But it's an intensity driven by his sheer love of the birds and the sport they provide.

Now, we all like to do it on our own. But I have to give credit where credit is due. Without these guys ... without the guides ... it's unlikely I'd have gained the wealth of experiences, (And I truly believe I'm a richer man for them), that I have.

CHAPTER THIRTY-FOUR

On Snow Geese

It's just human nature. We always long for that which is not at hand. Too often taking for granted that which is. Such was the case for me early on. While I never (and still don't) take our growing opportunity for Canadas lightly, snow geese separated themselves in my mind's eye as something rare and special.

In my youth flights of snows and blues were actually not uncommon in eastern Wisconsin. There always were a few days ... maybe a week ... come late October or early November, when the season's northeasterly gales would blow these birds off their migratory route along Lake Michigan, pushing them inland where they'd sometimes land to rest and feed. Lucky and envied among his peers was the hunter who could pull off a successful sneak and bag a trophy bird or two.

It seemed only natural, after devouring everything I could find to read about them, that I eventually found myself on the western prairies, hunting these magnificent birds where they were traditionally common. After no small amount of trial and error we began to have our occasional way with them, much to my delight.

Hunting whitey was and remains infectious for me. Beginning in the drought-stricken '80s the snows and blues provided many a memorable prairie hunt when the ducks simply couldn't. But the more I chased them the more I realized it wasn't all about the hunting or the shooting. It was about the bird itself.

Of all our waterfowl none, NONE, is as purely and instinctively wild as the white goose. Nesting in the remotest of regions at the top of the world and spending the rest of the year on the move, migrating up and down half of it, the snow goose will never be found on a golf course, or eating popcorn in a lakefront parking lot. Surviving and proliferating in the face of such adversity as the harshest of weather conditions and nearly year-

around hunting, is not only remarkable, it's hard to comprehend the instinctive staying power of this wonderful creature. It speaks to a sheer will that humankind should only hope to emulate.

When I first heard Tony Dean reverently refer to the snow goose as "The Wild One," I thought, "How appropriate!" But the more time I spent in pursuit of this ever-more-challenging bird, the more I came to understand what he meant. To marvel at the simple magnificence of a flight of snows and blues is to contemplate the mystery of life itself.

To those who curse the white goose, and refer to it in such derogatory terms as "sky carp," just because they find the hunting too difficult or frustrating, I say, "Shame on you!" Whether it's snow geese or any other of God's great creatures, you just don't get it!

While there's really nothing in our world of wildfowling quite like a fast and furious snow goose shoot, the fact is they are the exception rather than the rule. That these eminently wild birds "win" more often than not, that they routinely humble us, is, it seems, as it should be.

CHAPTER THIRTY-FIVE

Looking Ahead

My life as a wildfowler, thanks to a good foundation, good friends, and good fortune, has exceeded all my expectations and dreams. While I eagerly anticipate the good times ahead, if it all ended today, I'd have no regrets, no complaints. The fact is however, there has flowed a lot more water under my waterfowling bridge than there will in the future.

Looking ahead now, I can see it off in the distance. It's that closet. That once wonderful, now damned basement hallway closet. Its door is hanging open. Now crammed with wonderful memories, there appears precious little space, but it looks like just enough, in which to stow the gun, the gear, the heart, and the soul of this enthusiast, one last time.

Sadie